COREY RUSSELL
PURSUIT OF THE
HOLY

Kansas City, Missouri

ForerUNNer BOOKS (F)

Pursuit of the Holy
By Corey Russell

Published by Forerunner Books
International House of Prayer–Kansas City
3535 East Red Bridge Road
Kansas City, Missouri 64137
(816) 763-0200 Ext. 675
www.IHOP.org

ISBN-13: 978-0-9776738-9-6
ISBN-10: 0-9776738-9-8

Cover design by Owen A. Brock, Visual Fluency
Interior design by Dale Jimmo

Printed in the United States of America

Dedication

This book is dedicated to the memory of A.W. Tozer and Leonard Ravenhill, who labored tirelessly to see the knowledge of the glory of the Lord fill the earth "as the waters cover the sea" (Habakkuk 2:14).

TABLE OF CONTENTS

Foreword

More than thirty years ago, I read A.W. Tozer's book entitled *The Knowledge of the Holy* and a book by J.I. Packer called *Knowing God.* The reality of God these books describe created a deep hunger in me for the knowledge of God. I began to ask, "Who is God? What is He really like? How do I find Him? How can I know Him? How can I have living understanding of Him?"

Knowing *about* God was no longer acceptable. I wanted to know *Him* intimately, personally, experientially. I began to search everywhere for God. I devoured the Bible and cried out in prayer. I was desperate. My longing to know Him was so intense, it was painful. But I knew I couldn't be satisfied by anything else. I had to know Him.

One day when I was reading Proverbs 2:1-5, I had a revelation. Proverbs 2:1-5 makes it clear that the knowledge of God and the understanding of the fear of the Lord are released by God to those who commit to searching for these treasures. He is looking for voluntary lovers: people who long to know Him more than anything else; people who will live lifestyles of prayer, fasting and meditation on the Word of God because they hunger to know a holy God; people who will seek the knowledge of God because they want to be transformed and invited into the deep things of God's heart.

I've come to understand that this invitation is for all of us—yes, even weak, sinful ones like you and me. We can all know God because He created us and redeemed us through the cross for that purpose. He saved us so we could know Him and be in relationship with Him. And it is by knowing God and being in relationship with Him that we are transformed. That is why the Proverbs 2 pathway is so important. We are meant to find our strength and redemption in God alone. The knowledge of God is the secret to transformation and intimacy with God.

Jesus has always invited men and women to pursue Him. Matthew 5:6 records Jesus saying, "Blessed are those who hunger and thirst for righteousness, for they shall be filled." He also said, "Ask, and it will be given to you; seek, and you will find; knock, and it will be opened to you. For everyone who asks receives, and he who seeks finds, and to him who knocks it will be opened" (Matthew 7:7-8). Matthew 7:7-8 tells us what to do. Matthew 5:6 tells us why we should do it. And Proverbs 2:1-5 tells us how to do it. Proverbs 2:1-5 instructs us how to go about finding God and the knowledge of Him.

Pursuit of the Holy is an excellent book. It examines and unfolds Proverbs 2 in a clear, concise manner that is both inspiring and enlightening. Corey Russell accurately describes the lack of the knowledge of God in the Church at large and explains why it is vital that we address this lack and change our focus accordingly. He then humbly offers practical and helpful insight about how to do so. Corey guides us down the Proverbs 2 path of finding the knowledge of God and shows us the importance of knowing God. The Church's greatest need in this hour is for shepherds after God's heart who can feed others on the knowledge and understanding of God (Jeremiah 3:15). I believe that God is raising up a generation of shepherds throughout the earth who will walk in living understanding of God. This book will be a tremendous asset to them.

Corey Russell has faithfully given himself to the pursuit of the knowledge of God. In his teaching, in his public life, in his family life, and in his spiritual life, he embodies the realities set forth in this book. Corey, one of the favorite teachers at our Bible school and an associate director of our Onething young adult internship, is committed to training young adults. He has been gripped by God, consumed by the vision of raising up young men and women who will give up everything to know God. I pray that, as you read this book, you will be stirred as well and will begin to cry out for the knowledge of God. He is not a distant, uncaring God. He wants to be known, and He can be known. He is waiting for you to seek Him out.

Mike Bickle
Director of the International House of Prayer
Kansas City, Missouri

Introduction

The Church in America has a problem. The statistics that once differentiated the Church from the world no longer do. The same problems that are crippling the world are now crippling our churches. Divorce rates in the Church equal those of the world. Pornographic addictions in the Church compare to those outside the Church. There is burnout in the ministry; pastors and leaders are leaving churches because of scandal, immorality or boredom. And we are on a head-on collision course with the most important hour of human history.

Do we need one more idea, one more technique, one more new way to evangelize the lost? Do we need one more new way to do anything? No. What we need is to get to the root of these issues. The greatest problem we have in this day is that we do not know who God is or what He is feeling. A.W. Tozer wrote in *The Knowledge of the Holy*, "All the problems of heaven and earth, though they were to confront us … at once, would be nothing compared with the overwhelming problem that we have with God: that He *is*; what He is *like*; and what we as moral beings must *do* about Him"

(p. 2). He said that ten thousand lesser problems would be solved when we come to a right understanding of God (p. 2).

The greatest problem for the Church in this nation is not a sin problem as we would typically think of sin. Rather, it is the subject of God—who He is, what He's like, and who are we to Him. Our mandate is to know Him intimately, yet we do not understand who He is. We show up at church one day a week, throw our money into a bucket and listen to what the man or woman of God has heard lately. We would rather do this than deal with what we truly believe about God.

We live in a time similar to that of Hosea, who cried out, "There is no truth or mercy or knowledge of God in the land" (Hosea 4:1). The knowledge of God that I'm talking about goes way beyond just being able to spit out facts that we've known about Him for as long as we've been alive. I'm talking about intimate, living knowledge of God that dwells in the core of our beings. It's time to sound the alarm like Hosea did. It's time to call the Church to return to the knowledge of God.

Right now so many Christians are running around, looking for the newest method of evangelism, the newest format for cell groups, the newest this and the newest that, all in the hopes of solving our problems and avoiding judgment. Where is the awe, the wonder, the silence that our fathers knew in the face of God? Today, what we know about God does not translate into transformed lives—it does not re-establish worship and prayer, and it does not result in people walking in the fear of the Lord. The true knowledge of God surpasses words and takes us into the very life of God Himself, transforming us and causing us to live like people from another age.

God is calling out to a generation to "lift up your eyes ... and see who has created these things" (Isaiah 40:26). It's time for us to come up higher, to lift our gaze higher, to gain an eternal perspective, and to touch God for real. We must unlearn many things we think we know about the Father, about the Son, and about the Spirit, and ask for fresh revelation that brings us into true reality.

In light of the hour of history in which we live and of the landscape of the Church and nation, our one hope of receiving mercy is to return to the Lord through prayer and fasting. Hosea and Joel gave the same cry to their people. Hosea called to his generation, "Come and let us return to the Lord ... Let us know, let us pursue the knowledge of the Lord" (Hosea 6:1,3). Joel pleaded with his generation to turn back to the Lord "with fasting, with weeping, and with mourning. For He is gracious and merciful, slow to anger, and of great kindness; and He relents from doing harm" (Joel 2:12). When the subject of God is restored as the primary ministry, application and proclamation of the Church, we will witness the greatest move of God the earth has ever seen.

The way into the knowledge of God is laid out in Proverbs 2. Solomon makes it clear that we will find the knowledge of God and understand the fear of the Lord (Proverbs 2:6) if we embrace a lifestyle of prayer, fasting and meditation on the Word of God. This lifestyle is not too difficult and not too mysterious. It's laid out for children and for the uneducated to follow. Jeremiah called the disciplines of this lifestyle "the ancient paths" (Jeremiah 6:16). He declared that if we found these paths, we would find rest for our souls.

To return to God, we must rediscover the God of the Bible, the God of our fathers, and the God and Father of our Lord Jesus Christ. To find the knowledge of God, we must take the Proverbs 2 path of wisdom. We must enter into a lifestyle and a lifelong journey ... *the pursuit of the Holy.*

CHAPTER

What Is the Knowledge of God?

What is the knowledge of God? What does it truly mean to believe in God? Is it a verbal and intellectual agreement with what we've been told our whole lives, or is it something much deeper that goes on in the core of our being and transforms our whole lives? And what has God revealed of Himself in the Bible? What has God revealed of Himself through the person of Jesus Christ?

These questions are more than fill-in-the-blank quiz questions. They should entice us and draw us into the mystery of God, where our mouths are shut, our eyes are opened and we can only whisper, "Holy, holy." These questions ought to lead us to Him. They indict us. They show us that we are indeed the clay and God is indeed the potter. God asked 110 questions of Job, the most righteous man in the earth (Job 39-41). After Job heard these questions, he said, "Behold, I am vile; what shall I answer You?" (Job 40:4). He continued, "I lay my hand over my mouth. I have heard of you by the hearing of the ear, but now my eye sees You" (Job 42:5).

The Knowledge of the Eternal God

The doorway into the true knowledge of God is the awareness that what you think you know is nothing compared to the reality of Him. The lack of this understanding produces the arrogance and flippancy with which most of us live our lives. We must begin by declaring, as Job's friend Elihu did, "Behold, God is great, and we do not know Him" (Job 36:26). A.W. Tozer said that our concept of God is "utterly beneath the dignity of the Most High God" (*The Knowledge of the Holy*, p. 2).

Our God and Father is the One who dwells in unapproachable light, the One who creates. Even with all we've been taught, we've still only heard the whisper of His voice and seen the edges of His ways. The reality of God exposes our bankruptcy and spiritual barrenness. We hate the mystery of God. It shows us to be who we are: weak humans made in His image. It humbles us and intimidates us, exposing our frailty.

God unnerves us because we can't just define Him and go about our merry way. He defies definition. He's indefinable, and this chafes us. He's outside our little world. Psalm 113:6 states that God has to humble Himself to behold the things in the universe. He is mysterious, He is transcendent, and when we look at Him, we cannot articulate what we are seeing. Dealing with mystery scares us to the core. We want something we can handle, something we can define and market to other people, but God won't be boxed in by our perceptions of Him.

Eternity unnerves us too, because we can't just throw a title on it and continue on with business as usual. Have you ever seriously considered the subject of the eternity of God? The eternal nature of God is highlighted from Genesis to Revelation. The reality that God is uncreated separates Him from everything that we know and see.

Humor me for a moment. Close your eyes and think of your father. Next, think of your grandfather. Then your great-grandfather, then your great-great-grandfather, and so on. When you come to

Adam, consider the question, "Who is Adam's father?" I hope we agree that it's God.

Now consider this: "Who is God's father? Who brought God into being?" Think about Genesis 1:1: "In the beginning, God..." When the beginning began, God was there, which means that He was before the beginning. If He was before the beginning, then when did He begin?

This is where you jump off the diving board of Genesis 1 into eternity. Those four words are the beginning of your journey into the abyss of "before the foundation of the world" that Jesus described in John 17:5 and John 17:24. Cry out with Moses, "From everlasting to everlasting, You are God!" (Psalm 90:2). Lose yourself in eternity past. Reach as far as your mind will let you and realize that you are as far from the end of time as when you began.

I imagine by now that your brain is fried, but let's go the other direction now, into the future. Consider the second coming of Jesus and His reign on the earth for a thousand years. Think about eternity breaking in to dwell with men and women on the earth. Meditate on eternal paradise and eternal damnation. The fear of the Lord may have begun to grip your heart as you realize how small you are and how big God is. Tozer quoted the hymn writer Frederick Faber: "Only to sit and think of God / Oh what a joy it is! / To think the thought, to breathe the Name / Earth has no higher bliss!" (p. 12). Some people think it is a waste of time to think such thoughts, yet this is our portion. We were made to know God deeply and intimately and to live our lives out of the overflow of this encounter.

This journey into eternity is more than a cool exercise to stretch our minds. It is the way we are transformed into people who are more fascinated by eternity and its values than we are by the fleeting pleasures of this age. Isaiah declared, "All flesh is grass, and all its loveliness is like the flower of the field ... The grass withers, the flower fades, but the word of our God stands forever" (Isaiah 40:6,8).

We need a good dose of eternity, the place where moth and rust do not destroy. We were meant to declare, as David did,

"Great is the Lord, and greatly to be praised; and His greatness is unsearchable" (Psalm 145:3). David didn't mean that we can't search it out. He meant that we have the everlasting privilege and occupation of searching out the knowledge and greatness of an infinite Lord.

We were formed to search out the depths of God. Touching the knowledge of God is what makes us tick, what causes us to be alive. When we understand what we were created for, life makes sense. Unfortunately, we have lost sight of our ultimate purpose.

Identity Crisis

We are in an identity crisis. We don't know who we are. We don't know why we're here. We don't know why we were created. We live with our eyes on the ground, just trying to obey the Lord and resist temptation and do good deeds, not realizing that the Lord wants His people to know Him, to understand His heart. He created us out of His desire for communion and fellowship with mankind. He intended that, through this communion, dominion over all the earth would be released to men and women. But we have lost sight of God's high vision for us. Instead, we're trying to find our own purpose in life.

The most common cry of most people is "I need to find my calling." What they mean is, "Why do I exist?" People live their whole lives in search of something that will bring them satisfaction, fulfillment, thrill, pleasure. Each of these desires is God-given, but how we go about fulfilling these desires is where the breakdown occurs. Most of us spend all of our time looking in the wrong places and attempting to fulfill our desires in wrong ways. The sad thing is that this frenzy characterizes the lives of the majority of church-going people.

The right job, the right spouse, the right children, the right house, or the right financial set-up can't fulfill us. What I'm talking about goes to the core of every one of us. If we take time to listen and diagnose the true question of our lives, then we are on our way to finding the answer. The question is not, "What do I think my calling is on this earth?" The true questions we ought to be asking are, "Why did God create me? What is my eternal calling?"

Every one of us, regardless of gender, occupation or age, is called to know God intimately and search Him out fervently with all that we are. We were made by God for God. Period. We were made to search Him out.

We truly need to understand that we are eternal creatures. Though we were born, we will never die. We were created and formed by an eternal God who formed us with an eternal vacuum inside of us that can only be filled by God. We were formed in God's image, made in His likeness, and given capacities and faculties to relate to the eternal God.

Think about Adam in the garden, undefiled by sin. Consider his ability to peer into the mystery of God. I imagine he heard inexpressible things, touched the untouchable, tasted and smelled eternity. God ordained this glory of intimate relation and communication for one purpose: to allow Adam to understand His heart and His ways so that he could govern the earth out of that knowledge. Angels do not have this glory. No other creature was formed in such a way that his internal makeup was designed to relate with God. Genesis 1 reveals that God's desire is to be intimately known.

God Wants to Be Known

The calling of every believer is to know God. This is more than knowing about Him or regurgitating facts about Him. We are meant to know Him in a deep, living, experiential way.

God wants to be known. God, who is completely self-sufficient and self-dependent, completely without lack in any way, poured Himself forth in creation for the purpose of being known. He made Himself known to Adam, Moses and the prophets. The pinnacle of God's revelation was in the person of Jesus Christ. In Christ, God unveiled His heart, His nature, His personality, His ways and His words. Jesus, the Word of God made flesh, is the very articulation and manifestation of the invisible God. He has declared the Father to us that we may know Him.

Through the One who proceeded from the bosom of the Father, we touch God. In Christ we see God's ways; we hear God's words; we come face to face with God. Even at the end of His ministry, Jesus had to remind His disciples, "He who has seen Me has seen the Father" (John 14:9). Think about this. When you see this 5'7" Jewish Man (I'm making up His height), you are seeing and hearing the Father. He is the one who came from the presence of the Father to declare the Father to us. In His last prayer, Jesus stated that He had declared to us the Father's name and would continue to declare it until something was awakened in the earth (John 17:26). He is the divine manifestation of the Father.

In fact, it was Jesus' claims of being the door—the way, the truth and the life—that provoked the Jews' violent hatred of Him. Because they did not believe Jesus, they did not know who He was, and because they did not know who He was, they did not believe. God came near in Christ and no one recognized Him or understood His speech. Because they were not intimate with God's word, they did not know Jesus.

Deception is creeping into the Church today and it's centered around the question, "Who is this Man Jesus?" We have watered Him down. We've questioned His claims of who He is and minimized His teachings about what it means to follow Him. The present-day Jesus is a hippie-looking dude who just wants everybody to get along and be happy.

That's not Jesus. Jesus came to bring division, not peace. Jesus came as a sword to reveal what was in the heart of man. And what was revealed is that mankind has an inner disagreement with—yea, even a hatred of—who God is and how He does things. "He came to His own and His own did not receive Him" (John 1:11). Today, we hear preachers and pastors deny the deity and historical existence of Jesus. We hear them question the reality of His death, resurrection and ascension. We hear them downplay His second coming and the events that will surround His return. Beloved, this is serious. This is what John referred to as the antichrist spirit—that which denies that Jesus is the Christ and that He has come in the flesh.

So how do we defend ourselves against this deceiving spirit? We defend ourselves by gaining living knowledge of God. Knowing Jesus involves much more than remembering the altar call we responded to ten or twenty years ago. Knowing Jesus means having an ongoing, ever-increasing, ever-deepening, personal relationship with a Man who is God. It involves striving, searching and sacrificing.

Paul, the mature apostle, told the Philippians that he had lost everything, but the thing he wanted most was to know Christ and be found in Him.

> Yet indeed I also count all things loss for the excellence of the knowledge of Christ Jesus my Lord, for whom I have suffered the loss of all things, and count them as rubbish, that I may gain Christ and be found in Him. (Philippians 3:8-9)

Paul urged the church of Colossi to seek "all the riches of the full assurance of understanding [and] the knowledge of the mystery of God, both of the Father and of Christ, in whom are hidden all the treasures of wisdom and knowledge. *Now this I say lest anyone should deceive you with persuasive words*" (Colossians 2:2-4, emphasis added).

This man preached Christ and Christ alone. Paul reached and strove to know Jesus; that's what he wanted above all else. He impressed upon all of his churches the necessity of knowing Jesus. He was clear that this pursuit should be their first priority. Doesn't that just cut us to the core of our little religious lives?

Revealing the Deep Things of God

How do we know Christ? Through the Holy Spirit. God sent us His Spirit, the third person of the Trinity, so that we might be led in the journey of knowing Christ more and more deeply and intimately.

The Holy Spirit is a person. We are invited, called even, to become acquainted with and develop a deep relationship with Him.

The night before Jesus was crucified, He made it clear to His disciples that it would actually be to their advantage for Him to leave. In His stead, Jesus would send the Holy Spirit to teach them and direct them to the ocean of truths that were presented during His earthly ministry. Jesus said:

> I still have many things to say to you, but you cannot bear them now. However, when He, the Spirit of Truth, has come, *He will guide you into all truth;* for He will not speak on His own authority, but *whatever He hears, He will speak;* and He will tell you things to come. He will glorify Me, for He will take of what is Mine and declare it to you. All things that the Father has are Mine. Therefore I said that He will take of Mine and declare it to you. (John 16:12-15, emphasis added)

Jesus sent the Holy Spirit, the Spirit of Revelation, to bring us into greater knowledge of who He is. God has made Himself known in Jesus, but He invites us and equips us to search Him out through the Holy Spirit who lives in us.

> And I will pray the Father, and He will give you another Helper, that He may abide with you forever—the Spirit of Truth, whom the world cannot receive, because it neither sees Him nor knows Him, but you know Him, for *He dwells with you and will be in you.* (John 14:16-17, emphasis added)

The day we said "Yes" to Jesus Christ as our Lord and Savior, He placed within us the very spirit of God as a down payment of the age to come, for the purpose of leading us into all truth concerning God, both the Father and the Son. The Holy Spirit now lives in us and His job is to lead us into revelatory knowledge of the Son, who reveals the Father.

Paul described the purpose of the Holy Spirit in 1 Corinthians 2:9-12. In verse 9, he said, "Eye has not seen, nor ear heard, nor have entered into the heart of man the things which God has prepared for those who love Him." When we read this portion of Scripture, we often stop with verse 9, thinking about that glorious day when we will encounter God. But Paul did not intend for us to stop there. To do so is to take verse 9 out of context. Paul continued:

> *But God has revealed them to us through His Spirit. For the Spirit searches all things, yes, the deep things of God.* For what man knows the things of a man except the spirit of the man which is in him? Even so no one knows the things of God except the Spirit of God. Now *we have received,* not the spirit that is from the world, but *the Spirit who is from God, that we might know the things that have been freely given to us by God.* (1 Corinthians 2:10-12, emphasis added)

The things that had not entered into the minds of the former prophets and saints of old—those to whom Paul was referring—were the sights and sounds of God, the encounters with God Himself. Paul lets us know that we have been given the Holy Spirit for the purpose of knowing the deep things of God. God has given us His Spirit so that we might know God the Father and God the Son. Our portion is to know God, not from a distance, but in a real, tangible, living, intimate way.

The Holy Spirit's occupation is to search out the depths of God and make them known to us. The Holy Spirit is constantly hearing things, and His job is to make those things known to us. I picture the Trinity in conversation with one another. The things that the Spirit hears, He makes known to people who are hungry to know the secret things of God. Jeremiah 31:34 says, "They all shall know Me, from the least of them to the greatest of them." This Scripture alone is proof that God wants us to know Him, that we can know Him. It's time to call the Body of Christ to its glory, to know and to fellowship with God in the Spirit.

Paul prayed for the Ephesian church, asking the Lord to give them *"the spirit of wisdom and revelation in the knowledge of Him, the eyes of your understanding being enlightened*; that you may know what is the hope of His calling [and] what are the riches of the glory of His inheritance in the saints" (Ephesians 1:17-18, emphasis added). The Spirit of Revelation is the Holy Spirit, who moves upon the hearts of His people. Through the Word, the Spirit makes known to our hearts who God is.

Friends of God

We are called to understand the revelation of God. If we do not know who He is, we will be like the people in Jeremiah's time. Jeremiah's generation was on the brink of judgment because they did not know God. They had become deceived. They had experienced a time of prosperity and peace in their land, and had misinterpreted God's mercy, thinking God was winking at their wrongdoings and blessing them anyway. God, in His great mercy and compassion, was actually giving them time to repent, rather than being indifferent to their sin.

A similar deception marks many of our lives and our congregations today. The heart question in this generation is the same heart question as in the days of Jeremiah. What are you confident in? Are you confident in your gifting, your ability, your resources, your contacts, your affiliations and your finances? Or are you confident in your God? Are you confident that you understand what is going on in the heart of God for your generation?

> "Let not the wise man glory in his wisdom, let not the mighty man glory in his might, nor let the rich man glory in his riches; but let him who glories glory in this, that he understands and knows Me, that I am the Lord, exercising lovingkindness, judgment and righteousness in the earth, for in these I delight," says the Lord. (Jeremiah 9:23,24)

God is crying out, "Who understands Me? Who knows what is going on in My heart? Who feels what I feel as I prepare to send judgment? Who has a clue about the tenderness in My heart?"

We are called not only to know God, but to teach others to know God. Jeremiah prophesied that God would give His people shepherds who would feed them with the knowledge and understanding of Him (Jeremiah 3:15). I believe God is in the process of raising up friends who know Him deeply and intimately, who will walk with Him and carry His heart, and who will share His heart with others. I really believe that God is causing the body of Christ to transition from having a servant mentality to having a friendship mentality. Jesus said, "No longer do I call you servants, for a servant does not know what his master is doing; but I have called you friends, for all things that I heard from My Father I have made known to you. You did not choose Me, but I chose you and appointed you that you should go and bear fruit, and that your fruit should remain" (John 15:15-16).

Knowing God is about more than having information. It is about who can and who cannot be trusted with the deep things of God's heart. The Lord rocked my paradigm about four years ago concerning what it means to be a friend of God. I have always longed to be one of those intercessors who stayed up all day and all night in intercession, like David Brainerd. The problem was that I never could wake up in the middle of the night. A burglar could have come in and robbed the whole house, and I would have slept through it.

My big night eventually came, though. The Lord woke me up supernaturally at 3:00 a.m. My eyes popped open and I heard the Lord say, "Get up. I want you to be with Me." I wanted to get up, but I told him I was tired and went back to sleep. Five minutes later, He woke me up again, and I responded the same way. Five minutes after that, the Lord spoke to me a third time and asked, "Can you not tarry with me one hour?"

I said, "Okay, I'll get up! I'll get up!" You can't go back to sleep after hearing that verse (Mark 14:37).

I went into another room and waited. I was sure I was going to hear some supernatural revelation that would impact the nations.

It seemed to me that if God had awakened me, the intercessor, He must have something important to say. There must be something big going on. I sat in that room for fifteen minutes, waiting with my notepad in hand, but nothing happened. I began to doze. In time I went back to sleep.

I woke up the next morning frustrated and angry. My big chance had come and I had messed it up. I went to the International House of Prayer and spent the first hour in the prayer room being upset with myself. Eventually I decided to share what had happened with one of my good friends and ask if she had any advice.

After I told my friend what happened, she looked at me and said, "Don't you know what He wanted from you, Corey? All He wanted was for you to be with Him. He didn't need you to do anything or to pray anything. He wanted you to be with Him because He counts you as His friend."

Those few phrases shook my whole concept of God and of how He sees me. I realized that I have value to Him and that I bring comfort to His heart. That realization is massive. And it's a hammer blow to the spirit of religion that defines us by what we do, rather than by who we are. That encounter led me into the understanding that God wants me, not because of what I do for Him, but because of who I am to Him. He who inhabits eternity values us because we are His friends. In the next chapter, we will examine this mystery.

CHAPTER

Tasting Eternity

Knowing God is our portion. It's what we were made for. But we have to lay groundwork before we can jump into the pursuit of knowledge. Two thousand years ago, Jesus asked His disciples two questions. He is asking us the same questions today.

Who Is This Man?

The first question Jesus asked was, *"Who do men say that I, the Son of Man, am?"* Jesus deliberately asked this question to determine if the disciples had based their revelation of Him on what others said about Him. I believe the greatest hindrance to our having real revelation of Christ is living on what others have told us about Him, instead of pursuing personal revelation of Him. Most of us base our thoughts and ideas of God on what our parents, siblings, friends, pastors, youth leaders, or Sunday school teachers said about Him. We settle into a false complacency; we pride ourselves on having knowledge, not recognizing that we lack the power of knowledge in our inner man.

The second question Jesus asked was, *"Who do you say that*

I am?" What a question. This is not a question we can answer immediately and without thought and then forget about. It is a heart-searching, heart-wrenching and heart-gripping question. Let us not, in our arrogance, think we know the answer. I'm convinced we do not know who Jesus is. The answer to this question will not be worked out at church one Sunday or at home-group on a Wednesday evening. Our answer will be worked out over years as we go on the journey of seeking and pursuing the revelation of the knowledge of God. We can't gain this knowledge on the run or through casual, haphazard seeking. Do this: sit down and list all the verses about God you've ever learned in your life. After fifteen minutes, let's take a look at your list and then let's talk.

The first step to knowing Jesus is admitting that we can't understand Him on our own. Paul was overcome with the mystery of this Man. He stated in Ephesians 3:8 that he needed supernatural help to even talk about Jesus. Hans Urs von Balthasar wrote in his book, *Prayer,* "Anyone contemplating the life of Jesus needs to be newly and more deeply aware every day that something impossible, something scandalous has occurred: that God, in His absolute Being, has resolved to manifest Himself in a human life" (p. 159). We, as Christians, must feel the ground underneath us giving way. We must be overwhelmed with non-comprehension as we stare at this mystery of Godliness. As Paul said, "God was manifested in the flesh!" (1 Timothy 3:16).

In Matthew 16:26, Simon Peter answered Jesus' second question. It appears he wasn't really even paying attention to the questions, yet out of nowhere, he suddenly exclaimed, "You are the Christ, the Son of the Living God!" He was declaring that this man was the Messiah, the very expression of the uncreated God. This was an amazingly astute observation, especially from someone like Peter, a hot-headed guy who didn't know all that much and who often spoke before he thought.

Jesus responded, "Blessed *[or to be envied]* are you, Simon Bar Jonah, for flesh and blood has not revealed this to you, but My

Father who is in heaven" (Matthew 16:17, parenthetical comment added). He made it clear that Peter had not understood this through his own efforts or intelligence, but by revelation from the Father. The Father gave Peter supernatural revelation about Jesus.

Jesus went on to explain that the revelation of Himself was the foundation the Church would be built upon. On this foundation, true authority would rest.

> And I also say to you that ... *on this rock (your revelation of Me) I will build My church,* and the gates of Hades shall not prevail against it. *And I will give you the keys of the kingdom of heaven,* and whatever you bind on earth will be bound in heaven, and whatever you loose on earth will be loosed in heaven. (Matthew 16:18-19, emphasis and parenthetical comment added)

This passage gives clarity about the foundation on which we are to build our lives. The foundation is our wrestling with the question, "Who do you say that I am?" and our striving to find the answer. This is not a one-time question with a one-time answer. It is something that is fleshed out over time as we come to terms with who this Man truly is. We must begin to grapple with these foundational realities.

Jesus talked about two houses in Matthew 7. One of the houses was built upon sand and the other was built upon rock. When the rains came and the winds blew upon the house of sand, the house fell. When the storm came against the house built upon the rock, the house stood. We have to build our lives on a solid base: the knowledge of God and the revelation of Jesus.

The person of Jesus Christ opens heaven to us. Through knowing Him, we are invited into the realm of eternity, to taste, to touch and to experience God Himself. It's in Christ that heaven comes to earth and earth is now able to reach to heaven. The wealth and riches of heaven are made available to us in Christ.

To know Christ is to love Christ. We are cold in our affections, our sacrifices, and our devotion because we lack the true revelation of Christ. When Jesus is truly revealed to us, we are awakened to love—love that causes us to forsake all the fleeting pleasures of this temporal age and throw ourselves into eternal things, into the age to come.

Growing in Love

How do we grow in love for God? This question set the stage for John 17:26. Jesus stated, "I have declared to them Your name, and will declare it, that the love with which You loved Me may be in them." I want to look at this verse by beginning at the end and working our way backward.

I'm blown away as I consider the implications of this phrase. Jesus, who has been consciously aware of the Father's pleasure in and affection for Him from before the foundation of the world, asked the Father to take this affection and place it in people who had not even been born yet. Jesus desired that those people would love Him the way the Father loves Him.

I have two questions in light of this verse. The first one is, "How much does the Father love the Son?" Let us not just say, "A lot," and move on. Let us allow ourselves to be brought into the mind-blowing reality of the eternal love between the Father and the Son through the Spirit. What manner of love! How boundless is it? How unchanging is it? The second question is, "What would your life and my life look like if we loved Jesus the way the Father loved Jesus?" What would we do differently? How would our priorities change? What would it look like for each of us?

Remember, this was Jesus, the second person of the Trinity, praying to the first person of the Trinity, asking the Father to touch a people and cause them to see and love Jesus in this way. Though the full implications of this verse will take eternity to uncover, Jesus prayed this prayer so that an unbelieving world would see an indescribable quality in the Church and be inspired to put their faith in Jesus. It hasn't happened in the full measure yet, but it will.

How does God cause us to grow in love? We must look at the first phrase of this verse to find how this will happen. "I have declared to them Your name, and will declare it," Jesus said. The declaration of the name of God is the same thing as the spirit of revelation in the knowledge of God. It's the communication of God Himself.

In Exodus 33:18, Moses cried out for the Lord to show him His glory. In chapter 34, God descended on the mountain and declared the name of God. God, in essence, was saying, "So you want to see My glory? My glory is My name. My glory is who I am."

> The Lord descended in the cloud and stood with him there, and proclaimed the name of the Lord. And the Lord passed before him and proclaimed, "The Lord, the Lord God, merciful and gracious, longsuffering, and abounding in goodness and truth, keeping mercy for thousands, forgiving iniquity and transgression and sin, by no means clearing the guilty, visiting the iniquity of the fathers upon the children and the children's children to the third and fourth generation." (Exodus 34:5-7)

In the same way that God showed His glory and declared His name to Moses, Jesus declared the name and glory of the Lord to an entire generation. This is the way of awakening love in the earth: Jesus, being the brightness of the Father's glory, shows forth the glory of the Father. Every interaction, every word, every deed, every movement, every smile and every emotion from this Man brings us past the exterior and into the interior life of the uncreated God. We are given access into the Most Holy Place to gaze upon things which angels desire to look into (1 Peter 1:12).

Jesus proclaimed the name of His Father throughout His life. He proclaimed the Father's name as He hung upon that cross. He declared it at His resurrection and at His ascension. Now He sits at the right hand of God, interceding for us and declaring the Name again and again. He will continue declaring that Name until all believers are swept into the eternal love of the Godhead. He will declare it openly at His second coming when the glory of the Lord comes and all people see it.

We must grasp the importance of the knowledge of God. We were created to pursue this eternal knowledge with all of our hearts, souls, minds and strength. We were made to feast on the knowledge of God and to delve into the mysteries of His heart, His thoughts, His wisdom, His power and His goodness. Let the same cry of Moses come alive in this generation: "Show me Your glory!"

What Is the Knowledge of God?

We need be clear about what the knowledge of God is. The true knowledge of God does involve an intellectual agreement and a verbal agreement with who He is. But the knowledge of God goes way beyond that.

I would define the knowledge of God as the intimate spiritual knowing and understanding of Him. This knowing transcends the way we know our acquaintances or friends. It involves a deep and intimate knowledge of God. The word "know" in the Old and New Testaments carries with it the idea of a husband knowing a wife in a marriage relationship. This knowing is a deep sharing and interchange of words, thoughts, emotions and experiences; it surpasses a mere mental or verbal agreement.

In John 17:3, Jesus called the knowledge of God eternal life: "This is eternal life, that they may know You, the only true God, and Jesus Christ whom you have sent." Jesus defines eternal life not quantitatively, but qualitatively. He defines it not primarily as something that happens after we die; it is a quality of experience that is found when we come into contact with the only true God in this life. This experiential knowledge of God encompasses salvation, but is not limited to salvation. Nor is it limited to a one-time encounter with Him. It is, in fact, boundless. It involves an ever-growing, ever-increasing, intimate and living understanding of God. This is what the apostles prayed for and what is available to every believer: growing in the knowledge and revelation of God.

Jesus defines the realm of eternity as touching God in the Spirit. This is not some second-rate event for weak people who need experiences to increase their faith—the experiential knowledge of God is the foundation, the basis, the rock of our faith. We have tried to pit faith and emotional encounter against each other, but they are two sides of the same coin. They are inseparable. Every founder of the faith encountered something of the Spirit that launched them in the realm of faith. They endured because they saw Him who is invisible. As Hebrews 11:13 says, they saw the land that was afar off; they were assured of its reality. They embraced eternity and confessed that they were pilgrims and strangers on the earth.

Paul prayed that the church of Ephesus "would know the love of Christ which passes knowledge" (Ephesians 3:19). How could they know something which passes knowledge? Yet Paul prayed it and God caused it to be recorded in His Word, so it must be a real thing in the grace of God. Paul was talking about an experience with the love of God—something that surpasses our human capacity to comprehend and process, something supernatural. He was talking about a mystical encounter with God through the Holy Spirit.

Adam had continual revelation and encounter with God in the Garden of Eden before he and Eve sinned. What Adam knew and experienced of God before he sinned has been reinstated through the second Adam, Jesus, who ushered in greater righteousness, better promises, and greater access to God Himself through the Holy Spirit. We were made to feast on God, to get lost in God, to see, to hear, to encounter, to live in the realm of the Spirit.

I've heard the statement, "You're so heavenly minded that you're no earthly good." That is one of the most incorrect and misguided statements ever. You can be no earthly good *unless* you are heavenly minded. You are of no use to anyone if you do not have fresh understanding and awareness of the realm of the Spirit. We can't know how to assess situations or recognize truth if we don't have that kind of understanding.

Paul commanded the believers at the church of Colossi to set their minds on things above, where Christ is seated at the right hand of God (Colossians 3:1-3). Setting our minds is not a casual, I-will-get-around-to-it-next-week attitude—it is a deliberate, focused resistance to anything that stands in the way of us getting rooted in God and the things of God. Paul was saying our life on earth isn't the extent of our life; that, in reality, we are seated with Christ in heavenly places, and our true identity is found in accessing, even living in, the realm of the Spirit. This is a completely foreign idea to most Christians.

It's About Fascination

We are a bored generation. We get much more excited about the newest Hollywood flick or latest video game than we do about the Word of God or His invitation to enter the realm of the Spirit. When I speak to groups of people, I usually have them repeat after me, "God's not boring, I'm boring!" While we were created by God with appetites for pleasure and fascination, we have completely lost sight of where real, authentic pleasure and fascination are found. The truth is that we no longer even have appetites for real pleasure or real fascination. We've settled for inferior pleasures for so long that most of us don't even know what we're missing. We are half-hearted creatures who don't know what we were made for.

We were made to be stunned at the sights and sounds of heaven. God means for us to be awestruck by His ways and overwhelmed by who He is. This is not a hard-to-attain way of life, meant only for a select few. This is the portion of everyone who has been redeemed by royal blood. John 1:14 states, "And the Word became flesh and dwelt among us, and we beheld His glory." We are meant to be amazed and captivated by His glory. We can't even imagine what He has in store for those who seek Him out. As Paul said, quoting the prophet Isaiah, "Eye has not seen, nor ear heard, nor have entered into the heart of man the things which God has prepared for those who love Him" (1 Corinthians 2:9).

Have you read Ezekiel 1 in a while? When Ezekiel was in

Babylon, he saw an open vision in the sky. The vision was of God on His throne. He saw a whirlwind of fire with living creatures shooting back and forth through the whirlwind like flashes of lightning. He witnessed a "firmament," the sea of glass described in Revelation 4:6. Ezekiel described a Man made of fire sitting on the throne who spoke to him. In the first of several encounters, the Lord fed him a scroll (gave him a prophetic message), talked with him and commissioned him to speak to the nation of Israel.

The Bible says that Ezekiel sat by the river Chebar for seven days after the vision, astonished! Everyone around him must have thought he'd lost his mind. He sat there speechless, staring off into the distance for a week. Has that ever happened to you after watching a good movie or playing a good video game? I doubt it. What Ezekiel experienced—now that's what I call fascination!

The prophets weren't the only ones astonished by God and His eternal nature. Paul was writing to Timothy about pastoral issues when, out of nowhere, he wrote, "Great is the mystery of godliness: God manifested in the flesh!" (1 Timothy 3:16). It's like he was writing away about the qualifications to be a deacon, and he was suddenly struck by the magnitude and magnificence of Jesus becoming a Man. Paul was apparently stunned again as he penned the Book of Romans. Near the end of his great discourse on the mystery of Israel and the Church, he suddenly broke out in a rapturous declaration: "Oh, the depths of the riches of both of the wisdom and knowledge of God! How unsearchable are His judgments and His ways past finding out!" (Romans 11:31).

These are more than doctrinal truths we are meant to agree with. They are marvelous, mysterious realities that should cause us to fall on our knees and worship God. God never intended for us to just get information clear in our minds—He intended for us to be fascinated by Him for all of eternity. It's about being stunned over and over again. If our information about God is not accompanied by wonder, something is wrong. We must go unlearn what we have been taught about God so we can learn the truth about Him.

Let's be honest. What causes us to marvel? What fascinates us? What causes us to weep? Are we stunned at the beauty and knowledge of God when we read the Word of God, or are we fascinated with everything but the Word of God?

The Battle for the Eyes

We were made to look into, to gaze upon and to consider the beauty of the Lord. We were meant to join David in saying, "One thing I have desired of the Lord, that I will seek: that I may dwell in the house of the Lord all the days of my life, to behold the beauty of the Lord, and to inquire in His temple" (Psalm 27:4). We were made in the image of God and according to the likeness of God, to relate with the uncreated One. God created mankind as the only creature who could commune with Him. Our eyes were made to see God, our ears to hear God, our hands to touch God, our senses to encounter God. What was it like to see God walking in the garden when heaven and earth were one? How did Adam see God before sin came into the equation?

Jesus made it clear that the eye is the lamp to the body (Matthew 6:21-23). If the eye is good, the whole body is good, but if the eye is bad, so is the whole body. What we open our eyes to is what we open our souls to. This is the beholding/becoming principle of Scripture: we become like that which we behold. In 2 Corinthians 3:18, Paul stated, "But we all, with unveiled face, beholding as in a mirror the glory of the Lord, are being transformed into the same image from glory to glory, just as by the Spirit of the Lord." If our eyes behold the things of God, we will be transformed into godly people and we will hunger for more of God. If we behold evil and perverse things, our souls will be filled with those perversions and we will never be satisfied.

Pornography is a billion-dollar industry in America, and its production and use are increasing at alarming rates. Thousands of pornographic films are filmed every month. The pornography produced in this country not only defiles America, it defiles the nations of the earth. It lures our gazes away from God, away from true pleasure. There is a massive battle for our eyes—the lamps to our bodies—and we need to wake up and fight it. We need to remember that we will become like whatever we behold. My cry is: "Enlighten my eyes, lest I sleep the sleep of death" (Psalm 13:3).

The beholding/becoming principle is why Paul emphasized the eyes in his prayer for the Ephesians: "That the Father of Glory may give to you the spirit of wisdom and revelation in the knowledge of Him, that the *eyes of your understanding may be enlightened*" (Ephesians 1:17-18, emphasis added). Where are the eyes of this generation? Where are your eyes? Where is your gaze? What are you beholding? What—or who—are you becoming like?

My life has been profoundly impacted over the last six years by two prayers in Psalm 119. The first one is in verse 18, where David cried out, "Open my eyes, that I may see wondrous things from Your law." It's time for wonder to be restored to the Church. It's time we exchanged stale, emotionless theories about God for authentic experience of God. The wondrous things of God should be the focus of our gaze.

The other prayer that has impacted me is in verse 37 of Psalm 119: "Turn away my eyes from looking at worthless things, and revive me in your way." David not only wanted to have his eyes opened up to the wondrous things of God; he also wanted his eyes closed to the worthless things, the things not of God. Worthless things are not just things like pornography. They are the things we might consider permissible. David was, in essence, saying, "Remove even the things that look harmless or even good to make more room for You in my soul."

"Good" is the worst enemy of "best." All of this is about more than PG- versus R-rated movies. It's about really considering what takes up room in our souls. Are we allowing space that could be filled by the knowledge of God to be occupied by lesser things? So often we secretly congratulate ourselves for not engaging in pornography or some other blatant sin, without understanding that the twenty-five PG movies we watched in a week rob us of God just as effectively. These "harmless" things don't hurt us as much as sin, but they certainly don't contribute to our life in God. By the time we get around to the things of God in a typical week, we are so stuffed with all the "good" and "permissible" things that we have no room for God. So when we do spend time with Him, our experience in the Spirit is just as hindered as anyone else's.

The Church's approach to dealing with slavery to lesser things should not only be to pray for each other and break off spiritual oppression, but to get ourselves connected with that for which we were created: gazing on the beauty of God and looking into God Himself. It's not that our desires are too large; they are not large enough. We don't just want to cut off the bad fruit of sin. We want to gaze at real beauty: the God of the Universe.

Oh, for the spirit of revelation to touch us! We need the wonder of God restored, the beauty of God restored, the stunning fascination of encountering God restored, the beholding of God restored. We are blind, naked, wretched, miserable and poor, and we don't know it. Business continues on as usual in our churches, while the majority of our leadership teams are addicted to lesser things, to temporal pleasures, that are robbing our churches of the Spirit of revelation. There is no wonder any more in the pulpits, and there is no wonder in the congregations. We are bored stiff. We have no appetite for real pleasure or real beauty. We are defiled from gazing on the wrong things. We must wake up and address this.

We are living in a time like that described in 1 Samuel 3. There is no spirit of revelation. The lamp in the temple (the prayer ministry) is almost out. The voice of the Lord is calling out to a Samuel generation living in the midst of an Eli generation. The eyes of those in the Eli generation are so dim that they cannot see. God is scanning the earth for His seers, the ones who will soar in the realm of the Spirit to feast their eyes on God and perceive what He is doing.

Gazing on the Beauty Realm

There is a direct correlation between the raising up of a prophetic generation and what we gaze upon. God will surely raise up
burning and shining lamps, like John the Baptist (John 5:35). They
will burn because they have beheld the God who is ablaze with
desire, holiness and stunning majesty.

The beauty of God is described with overwhelming clarity and
power in Revelation 4. This passage invites us into what we in Kansas City call "The Beauty Realm." The apostle John received an
invitation to go up into heaven, into the place Ezekiel saw but did
not enter. He saw God sitting on that throne. The sights of God,
the sounds of God, the company surrounding God—they stunned
him.

Of all of the wondrous realities made known in this passage,
nothing strikes me as much as the living creatures who minister
before God. Of all the things God could have put around His throne,
He selected these weird-looking creatures with eyes all around
them and within them. Can you picture them? They have eyes on
their arms, legs, wings, backs, heads—everywhere. They are full of
eyes because they have one occupation: looking at God. That's it.
That's the only thing they've ever done throughout eternity.

These creatures are called "seraphim," which literally means
"burning ones." They are on fire as they gaze upon the burning
God. Out of continual encounter, they burst forth with descriptions
of God, singing, "Holy, holy, holy!" They never tire of their occupation or their singing. We usually get tired of the same worship song
after about a month; these guys have been singing the same worship song for millions of years.

Before we can feel the weight of what the seraphim are saying,
we need to examine the word "holy." Not only does it mean separation from everything impure, it means separation from *everything*.
God's holiness means He is transcendently above everything He
created. His mercy, His power, His wisdom, His goodness, His patience, His kindness, His justice, His righteousness and His love are

completely beyond anything created. This revelation of God is hitting the seraphim with such force that they cannot cease studying and praising the revelation of God. David declared in Psalm 145:3, "Great is the Lord, and greatly to be praised; His greatness is unsearchable." This doesn't mean God can't be known. It means we have an eternal occupation of searching out God, of entering into the realm and reality of His beauty.

I often picture these multi-eyed creatures gazing upon God. Every time they look at Him, they explode with joy and crash to the floor with overwhelming revelation of God, ecstatically declaring what He is like. I picture one seraph looking to another on the floor and saying, "Are you ready? Let's do it again!" They rise up and look at God again, and another facet of Him thunders across the heavenly temple.

I want to burn for God like John the Baptist, like the disciples on the road to Emmaus. Those disciples' hearts burned when they encountered Jesus. I'm convinced that God is going to raise up a burning people before His Son returns to the earth, just like He did at His first coming. Jesus desired to cast fire on the earth (Luke 12:49), and He is the One who came to baptize us in the Holy Spirit and fire. We have no fire in and of ourselves. We can't see the beauty realm of God on our own. We desperately need Him to give us vision so we can burn.

Vision for Revelation

To see is everything. Revelation causes faith to arise. Hebrews 11 describes how our fathers saw the land God promised them and how they saw the invisible God. This seeing launched them into violent lifestyles of faith in the midst of circumstances that seemed to testify against the reality of His promises. We must have a revelation of God, His heart, His ability, and our place before Him. Only then can we be launched into that level of faith.

In Revelation 4:1, John described hearing a voice from heaven that said, "Come up here, and I will show you things which must take place after this." John was immediately caught up "in the Spirit; and behold, a throne set in heaven" (Revelation 4:2). The word "behold" means that his senses were awakened to the realm of heaven. It's all about perspective. John had to get up there to heaven in order to understand the unfolding of the events he recorded in the rest of the Book of Revelation.

The Spirit of revelation is all about seeing. It "will guide [us] into all truth" (John 16:13) and awaken us to the realm of heaven. We must enter into the call to "come up here." I have heard the saying, "You can either pray from earth to heaven or from heaven to earth." I want to pray from heaven to earth. I want to pray from that realm, the realm of revelation, the realm of impossibilities, from the heavenly places with no boundaries and no hindrances. I want to pray from inside God's heart.

Paul prayed all of his prayers for his churches out of the overflow of his encounter with the knowledge of God. He told those in the Colossian church to set their minds, their affections and their realities in heaven. "If then you were raised with Christ, seek those things which are above, where Christ is, sitting at the right hand of God. Set your mind on things above, not on things on the earth" (Colossians 3:1-2). In essence, he was commanding them to answer the call to "come up here" like John did. He was saying that if they wanted vision, if they wanted power over issues in their lives, they had to get up there.

Luke 11 describes the disciples coming to Jesus and asking Him to teach them how to pray. Jesus made it clear that who you pray to is more important than what you ask for. Jesus told His disciples that, before they could even begin to ask things from God, they had to get connected with "our Father in heaven" (Luke 11:2). Jesus often "lifted up His eyes to heaven" (John 17:1) before He prayed. What did He see? Where did He go? He was rooted in the God of Revelation 4, who sits in glory and majesty upon His throne. Jesus instructed His disciples to do the same, to pray from the place of understanding that reality. The prayer He taught them to pray—what we call the Lord's Prayer—is more than a nice prayer to be said at bedtime and before football games. It is a door to the realm of heaven and it contains the greatest secret to restoring the prayer movement. The prayer movement will usher in the second coming of Jesus Christ, but it has to be restored in order to do so.

What hinders us from tasting eternity through the reality of prayer? Why don't we pray? I spent years yelling at people, calling them to pray, but few ever did. After a few years, I began to understand that there was a bigger issue than people not wanting to come to prayer meetings. We are a prayer-less people. We are a prayer-less generation because we lack the knowledge of God. Many believers in this nation are shame-filled, guilt-ridden, and full of condemnation because they have false ideas about Him. To call them to prayer meetings is to call them to look their problem of not knowing God in the face. Most people don't want to face their problem, so they don't pray. I don't pray like I want to. You probably don't pray like you want to either. We don't pray because we do not know who God is. We need true understanding of God and His nature. In Chapter 3, we will look at the battle between the false knowledge of God and the true knowledge of God.

CHAPTER

The Battleground

We've taken the first couple of chapters to lay a foundation for understanding the true knowledge of God. The knowledge of God is about more than having a good quiet time or meditating on the Word once a week—it involves the manifestation of the life of God in and through us. The true knowledge of God is a powerful, experiential knowledge that goes much deeper than an intellectual agreement. For instance, if all believers had the true revelation of God as the Healer, we would witness a healing revival that would touch millions. Instead, we boast in a form of godliness, but deny the power of it in our lives and in our churches.

The Essence of Idolatry

There is a more serious problem than the abortions, than the murders, than the immorality, than the drug and alcohol addictions: it is the lack of the knowledge of God. And this lack of knowledge is rampant in our churches, from the pulpit to the pews.

The number one hindrance to knowing God is knowing *about* God. It's more poisonous than we could ever imagine. When we think we know God, we become settled in a false complacency. We think we know something of God, when in reality we don't know anything at all. We are worshipping our idea of God instead of God Himself. A.W. Tozer calls this the essence of idolatry, defining it as "the entertainment of thoughts about God that are unworthy of Him" (*The Knowledge of the Holy,* p. 3).

Jesus taught that the knowledge of God was the foundation for Christianity. Paul made it clear to the Corinthian church in his second epistle: "For the weapons of our warfare are not carnal, but are mighty in God for the pulling down of strongholds, casting down *arguments* and every high thing that exalts itself against the *knowledge of God*, bringing every thought into captivity to the obedience of Christ" (2 Corinthians 10:4-5, emphasis added). This is the battleground: what we truly believe in our hearts about God. This is where the enemy stages his greatest warfare. If the enemy wins here, he wins everywhere in our lives. And as the church goes, so goes the world.

Rivers of sin flow from polluted fountains. Our fountains become polluted by the false beliefs we have about God. Often the false beliefs are so buried under what we think we believe that we aren't even aware that our fountain has become polluted. We find ourselves in sin and we don't even realize how we ended up there. We might have a vague idea and we can perhaps point to the final decision that took us over the line. But how did we get that close to the line in the first place? It all goes back to what we believe about God in the core of our being.

Satan, the father of lies, has bombarded us with lies about God since we were born. Most of us struggle with false ideas about God's heart for us and lies that question His ability to deliver us. Most of these arguments have been reinforced by past experiences with parents or other authority figures who have directly or indirectly communicated to us that God is distant from us, detached from our circumstances, and unable to bring change or deliverance.

Our environment feeds us lies and wrong views, too. We live in a nation that has witnessed fifty million abortions over the last thirty years. Divorce, sexual perversion and promiscuity have steadily increased, both inside and outside the Church. Relationships are more broken and dysfunctional than ever. Faithfulness is no longer a value, love has become cheap and meaningless, and commitment is something that only lasts as long as everything is going well. I think we secretly believe that God relates to us in the same way that people relate to one another.

Though we may not be aware of it, our experiences and observations have caused us to have wrong paradigms about God, to misunderstand His heart for us and question His ability to help us. And our Christian lives have suffered because of it. In the same way that an improperly laid foundation weakens a building, our spiritual lives are weakened and can eventually crumble if they are not built on the foundational truths about God. We have reduced God to whatever idea of Him suits our current mood and have boxed Him in to fit our agenda. We have made a god in our own image. No wonder there is almost no healthy fear of the Most High in the Church any more. The only kind of fear found in most churches is the fear of man. There is little awe, little true worship, little holiness. We have made Him into a god that we can control and manipulate and use for our plans and ideas.

This deviation from the truth is tragic and devastating. A low view of God corrupts everything and destroys our ability to receive the full power of the Gospel. A low view of God relegates the incarnation of Christ, the whole life of Christ, the death of Christ, and the resurrection and ascension of Christ to Sunday school lessons. If we don't get back to the Bible and encounter the God of the Bible, we will not view the Word who became flesh with the appropriate reverence. We will instead consider Jesus to be just a good prophet or a good teacher. The god of the majority of contemporary Christians is not the one true God at all, but is a weak, impotent, haphazard guy who's just glad we show up at church each week. That is both heresy and deception.

"As a Man Thinks in His Heart ..."

Proverbs 23:7 states, "As a man thinks in his heart, so he is." A man is not what he says at church on Sunday or at home group on Wednesday. A man is what he actually believes. Let's get to the heart of the matter: what we truly believe about God in secret.

We think we already know God because we believe that we know Genesis 1 or John 3:16. When we reread those Scriptures, we think, "I already know this passage." In truth, we don't know anything. We simply have information. We have become experts at cramming the night before a test and regurgitating data the next day. But when we're asked about the material four days later, it's clear that we don't really know it. So often, that's how we approach our relationship with God. We do the things we are supposed to do to stay out of trouble and to demonstrate to other people that we're doing all the right things, that we're a "good Christian." But we don't really know God; the power of the things of God has not been written in our hearts. We don't have any true knowledge or belief.

The greatest issue the church faces today is unbelief. Unbelief is the heart condition of someone who has bought into lies concerning God's nature and heart. Unbelief has become deeply rooted in the hearts of men and women, and is destroying the foundations of our faith. Most of us haven't verbalized our unbelief. We might not even know it exists. But it does. It's there in our hearts. Psalm 14 says: "The fool has said in his heart, 'There is no God.'" Stephen Charnock, in his book, *Existence and Attributes of God*, described this reality as practical atheism:

> Men may have atheistical hearts without atheistical heads ... All outward impieties are the branches of an atheism at the root of our nature ... Those, therefore, are more deservedly termed atheists, who acknowledge a God, and walk as if there were none, than those (if there can be any such) that deny a God, and walk as if there were one. (pp. 89-92)

Atheism of the heart allows us to sing the worship songs and quote the appropriate Bible verses, but the manifestation of the knowledge of God—or even the pursuit of it—in our lives is nowhere to be found.

Deception is the same as secret atheism. It occurs when we believe something to be true and that belief gives us our basis for reality. Paul told the Colossian church to seek "all riches of the full assurance of understanding, to the knowledge of the mystery of God, both of the Father and of Christ, in whom are hidden all the treasures of wisdom and knowledge. *Now this I say lest anyone should deceive you with persuasive words*" (Colossians 2:2-4, emphasis added). Paul's sole purpose in calling them to the knowledge of God was to enable them to not be deceived by what others told them about God.

We must begin to address the idolatry, the secret atheism and the deception that are rampant throughout the Church in this nation. Undeniably, we live according to what we truly believe. And right now, the lives of most Christians—even the well-meaning, compassionate, striving ones—indicate that they don't believe in the all-knowing, ever-present, all-powerful, holy, merciful, unconditionally loving, righteous God of the Bible. Multitudes in the Church confess (declare) truth, but their lives are a testimony of unbelief. Our hearts and our lives are divided. We say things with our mouths, but our hearts are out of touch with the reality of what we say. We listen to what others tell us about God, but our hearts and lives are not impacted. We try to fix the problems in our churches and families on our own and wonder why it doesn't work.

The situation brings to mind the Three Stooges trying to plug a leaking wall. A stream of water spurts out of one part of the wall. The stooges quickly put their fingers or hands over that leak. Then another stream of water comes out at another hole and they have to stick their other hand there. Then another leak springs, then another, then another, until all of their body parts are being used to plug the holes. Finally, the water cannot be held back any longer,

and the whole wall falls down. It seems we spend all of our time trying to plug the holes and stop the leaks, and we never deal with the
real problem: the lack of the true knowledge of God.

We've bought into lies concerning the majesty, the power, the
awesomeness of our God. These truths must be restored, because
if they are not, the impact of the Gospel on our spirits is significantly
weakened and the call to live sacrificial lives is ignored. We must
begin to wage war on our unbelief, on our distorted understanding
of God and on our lack of the knowledge of Him.

The good news is that we can fight back by rejecting our false
views of God. When we pursue the true knowledge of God through
prayer, fasting and meditation on the Word of God, the enemy's
power is weakened and our lives begin to manifest the life of Christ.
When the true knowledge of God breaks into our hearts, we will
live differently. When we sing, "Forever you are faithful, forever you
are true," and we believe it, it's not a just a song that we sing. We
will live differently. We will begin to give of our time, money and
resources in a radical way because we know God is faithful. We
will step out of our comfort zones because we know God will back
us up. We will be transformed. But in order for this to happen, we
must see God for who He is and feel the weight of His having taken
on our form in the person of Christ to reconcile us to Himself. The
revelation of the mystery of God will keep us from deception.

The writer of Hebrews declared that "without faith it is impossible to please God, for he who comes to God must believe that He is
and that He is a rewarder of those who diligently seek Him" (Hebrews
11:6). This scares me because it indicates that we can come to God
and not please Him. When we come to God, we must truly know His
heart. We must have a pure revelation of who He is as a rewarder.
How do we get that revelation? How do we enter into belief? We
have to ask the questions and we have to seek out the answers.
What does it mean to believe? Who is God? What is He like? How
does He feel? What is He doing? What is He thinking? What do we
look like to Him? Who is Jesus? Who is the Holy Spirit?

The questions are endless. And the answers won't be found at the next conference or in the next ministry line. They will be found as we humbly enter into a deep, probing search for them in the Word of God, and as the Word of God in turn reveals God to us. We have to go on this search by ourselves. Nobody else can do it for us. It's time for us to wean ourselves from depending on the revelations of other people. It's time to find out for ourselves who God truly is.

The Truth About God

"You thought that I was altogether like you," the Lord says (Psalm 50:21). "[But] as the heavens are higher than the earth, so are My ways higher than your ways, and My thoughts than your thoughts" (Isaiah 55:9). We are dealing with the Holy One of Israel, the Mighty One of Jacob. This is the One who spoke and the heavens were created, who spoke to the proud waves and gave them their boundaries, saying, "This far and no more." This is the God who confused the nations at Babel, who turned Egypt upside down, who led His people through the wilderness, who toppled mighty Assyria and mighty Babylon. This is the God who raised up a pagan king, Cyrus, to send God's people back home and to pay for rebuilding the temple. This is the God who does whatever He pleases (Psalm 115:3, 135:6).

Our God is the One to whom Moses cried out, "Who is like you among the gods, fearful in praises, glorious in holiness, doing wonders? You stretched out your hand and the earth swallowed them" (Exodus 15:11-12). He is the first and He is the last. He knows the end from the beginning. He is eternal, immutable, omnipotent, infinite, the God who has no beginning or end. He is the Rock from everlasting, the One in whom there is no variation or shadow of turning (James 1:17).

Our God is the Father of Glory, the Father of Lights, the Father of Spirit, and He is our Father who is in heaven. He is transcendent, far above all thought and all reason. The Lord is high above the nations, and His glory is above the heavens (Psalm 113:4). Wisdom and might belong to Him; He raises up kings and tears them down (Daniel 2:20-21). He humbles Himself to behold the things that are in the heavens and in the earth (Psalm 113:6). He is the One who sits above the circle of the earth, before whom the nations are like a drop in a bucket (Isaiah 40:15) and like grasshoppers (Isaiah 40:22). He is the God who sits in the heavens and He laughs at those who conspire against Him (Psalm 2:4). His kingdom and dominion endure forever (Daniel 4:3). Who is like our God? Who taught God anything?

> Who has measured the waters in the hollow of His hand, measured heaven with a span and calculated the dust of the earth in a measure? Weighed the mountains in scales and the hills in a balance? … With whom did He take counsel, and who instructed Him, and taught Him in the path of justice? Who taught Him knowledge, and showed Him the way of understanding? (Isaiah 40:12,14)

We need to understand who we're dealing with. Chapters 38-42 of Job describe God confronting a man with the truth of who God is and what He is capable of doing. He told Job, "Prepare yourself like a man and I will question you." God asked Job 110 questions about Himself, the I AM. These questions were a revelation of God's nature. Job's heart broke over his lack of the true knowledge of God and his inability to speak rightly about Him. Out of this new realization of God's majesty and his own poverty, Job said, "I have uttered what I did not understand, things too wonderful for me, which I did not know … I have heard of you by the hearing of the ear, but now my eye sees you" (Job 42:3,5).

Isaiah responded the same way after he encountered God in the Temple. He saw the Lord of Hosts sitting on His throne, surrounded by seraphim, filling the Temple with His glory. Isaiah said, "Woe is me, for I am undone! Because I am a man of unclean lips … for my eyes have seen the King" (Isaiah 6:5). Isaiah's response did not mean that he had a cussing problem. After seeing the glory and power of the Lord, Isaiah realized he was incapable and unqualified to speak rightly about God. He needed a supernatural coal touching his lips to enable him to speak about God rightly. That kind of revelation about God is the only remedy for our arrogance and pride, in both our personal and corporate lives.

Our God is the High and Lofty One who inhabits eternity, whose name is holy (Isaiah 57:15). Yet He is also humble. He is both majestic and tender. The God who is higher than the heavens is the same God who became a baby in a manger. The psalmist says,

> The Lord is high above all nations, His glory above the heavens. Who is like the Lord our God, who dwells on high, who humbles Himself to behold the things that are in the heavens and in the earth? He raises the poor out of the dust, and lifts the needy out of the ash heap. (Psalm 113:4-7)

Sometimes He seems untouchable to us, yet that quality is what gives weight to the revelation of Christ—the Word who became flesh (John 1:14). It should cause us to stand in awe, reverence, wonder and gratitude at what Jesus did by coming to earth as a human being.

Jesus' mission as "the Word of God" was to articulate, declare, and manifest the only true God (John 17:3). Jesus said, in essence, "You thought God was this way, but I have come to make it clear who He is and what He is really like." When Jesus touched the poor, the prostitutes, the sinners, He was telling us, "This is what God is really like." When He healed, when He delivered, when He spoke, He was unveiling the only true God. When He rebuked the Pharisees, he was making clear what God's heart was really about. Why did Jesus emphasize these things? Because He knew that the battles raging in our minds, emotions and souls revolved around the nature of God. The parables He told and the words He spoke were more than cool stories that we tell to our six-year-olds in Sunday school. Each one is a divine entrance and invitation into the eternal abyss of the uncreated God. They are doorways into the heart of the Father.

The Revelation of the Father's Heart

We are meant to know the Father. Jesus was constantly talking about knowing His Father. He said, "Not that anyone has seen the Father, except He who is from God; He has seen the Father" (John 6:46) and "As the Father knows Me, even so I know the Father" (John 10:15). Jesus told His disciples, "He who has seen Me has seen the Father" (John 14:9). In other words, when they looked at Jesus, they were seeing the Father. When they saw Jesus speak, touch, and feel, they were witnessing the Father's heart. Jesus' mission was to reveal to us what the Father is like, to impart in word and deed the intimate knowledge of God. His life demonstrated the Father's heart.

The story of the prodigal son that Jesus told in Luke 15 is about the revelation of God. Each one of us is the prodigal returning home to Him. We have wasted our lives living far away from Him, yet when God sees us, He feels compassion. He runs towards us, embraces us and kisses us. He meets us in our shame, in our nakedness, in our inability to work anything for our good or change anything for the better. That's the revelation of our Father: the God who looks past the stained-glass windows of our pretty religion and our frozen-on smiles and meets us right where we are, in the slums of our soul.

Do you evaluate your relationship with God based on how successful you were last week in your spiritual disciplines? On how many minutes you spent in your quiet time? On how much you fasted, or how long you prayed, or how engaged you felt in worship? On how much Scripture you memorized or the number of people you ministered to? Or do you evaluate your relationship with God based on the nature of your Father? We can't earn anything from God. And there is enough room in the Father's heart for weak people like Simon Peter, like us. Remember what Jesus told

Peter? "In My Father's house (*His heart*) are many mansions (*plenty of room*); if it were not so, I would have told you" (John 14:2).

The night before Jesus was crucified, He told the disciples that He was going somewhere they could not come. Peter longed to be with Jesus in that place, but wrongly supposed that his own ability could get him there. Jesus told Peter (and us) that he would fail miserably—but that in the midst of his failure, he would encounter the God whose commitment to Peter was stronger than Peter's commitment to God.

As Jesus had prophesied, Peter failed Jesus miserably by denying Him three times. We witness in John 21:15-19 God's heart for Peter, for us. After Jesus was resurrected, He came to Peter and asked him three times if Peter loved Him. Each time Peter said he did. Jesus then reinstated Peter as a leader. In the time of Peter's greatest failure, Jesus asked him if he loved Him and then restored him to leadership. What does that say about God's heart? Jesus chose a man who had denied his Messiah—not once or even twice, but three times—to become one of the most powerful preachers in Church history. This doesn't make sense to us. It's not how we would have handled the situation, but that's why the Lord gave us Isaiah 55:9: God's ways are above our ways. Knowing this should bring rest to our souls and hope to our hearts, even in seasons of weakness and struggle.

The prayer movement must be rooted in the knowledge of the Father's heart and founded on the righteousness of Jesus Christ alone. We live differently when we understand that, by grace, we already live in the place where we long to be—the Father's heart. Jesus crucified made this possible. In the Father's heart, we find rest, peace, joy and love. Having these enables us to live in confidence before God. Most Christians are fear-driven and guilt-ridden because of yesterday's mistakes, and they think they must make up for it to God. But the Father is not performance-based. He's not looking for us to make it up to Him. We couldn't make it up to Him anyway. He's looking for us to confess our sin, receive His forgiveness and be done with it so we can enter into intimacy with Him. He wants repentance unto relationship. It's the *relationship* He's after. That's why Jesus died—to restore the relationship between God and man.

I was saved nine years ago during a sovereign visitation of the Lord. In my town of three thousand people, more than a hundred high school students were saved. God moved greatly in my town for about six months and used me powerfully as a preacher and leader. I loved God very much, but during the second year after I was saved, I began to struggle with an area of sin. I struggled with it for more than six months. I cried every day over my weakness and over the disappointment I felt I was causing the Lord.

Eventually, that season of my life ended. After I stopped struggling with that sin, I told the Lord that I would never disappoint Him again. I was ashamed of my weakness and removed that entire season from my testimony. Over the next two years, I went on two 40-day fasts, prayed for two to four hours a day, and went hard after the things of God. What's sad is that I was motivated by fear, not love. What I did wasn't wrong; my reason for doing it was wrong. I felt I could not let up in my pursuit of God because I was afraid I would mess up again if I slowed down at all. I was constantly driven and made those around me miserable.

Four years after my struggle with that sin, I found myself in Norway on a ministry trip. I was alone almost eight to ten hours a day for a week. During that week, the Father cornered me and began to walk me through the story of Peter—how he denied the Lord, and how the Lord met him in the midst of his utter failure and welcomed him back with open arms. I began to understand that, like Peter, I had failed God miserably. Yet the Father's desire to welcome sinful men and women back with open arms had not diminished during the time between Peter's failure and mine.

As the Lord brought my season of struggle before me, He made something very clear: my season of failure would bring about a revelation of the Father's love for me that would be more powerful than the revelations of all my other seasons combined. I realized that all the fear-driven effort and anxious energy I had expended trying to make up for my failure had been worthless. God and God alone had always been my only hope of salvation. Salvation is not granted according to our spiritual achievement records. It's based on the righteousness of the Father and our acceptance of the forgiveness He grants us because of what Jesus did on the cross.

I came out of that week drastically changed and finally able to enter into rest. I came to terms with the fact that the Father's commitment to me was much stronger than my commitment to Him would or could ever be.

The Reality of the Father's Love

The majority of believers live with guilt, shame and condemnation because of past, and even present, seasons of sin. And it is destroying us. Are we only beautiful to God when we have it all together? If that were true, none of us would ever be beautiful to Him. Who among us doesn't have areas in our life in which we need help? If we had to fix every area of our life before we could be accepted by God, nobody would ever qualify for God's acceptance.

We must begin to hear and share about the real God, the One who is dedicated to calling us forth into maturity even as we struggle with areas of weakness. God doesn't just endure us during those seasons. He enjoys us as we reach for Him and cry out for Him in our struggles. Please understand that I am not talking about people who take the grace of God for granted and continue to sin, figuring God will forgive them, so why stop? Those people are on dangerous ground and are in real danger of Hell. I'm talking about believers who come up short because of their weakness and sin, but who long for God with every fiber of their beings and strive to be obedient to Him. As God strengthens them and loves them in the midst of their struggle, these weak ones come forth with powerful testimonies and revelation about God, which enables them to run the race steadily and tenaciously for decades. This is what our God is like. This is our Father. He really is that kind, that gracious, that tender, and that committed to us, even in our weakness.

One of the main obstacles to receiving the Father's love is fear. Whether we fear rejection or abandonment or authority figures, we live the majority of our lives afraid of what God really thinks and feels about us. Only one thing casts out fear: perfect love.

> What shall we say to these things? *If God is for us, who can be against us?* He who did not spare His own Son, but delivered Him up for us all, *how shall He not with Him also freely give us all things? Who shall bring a charge against God's elect?* It is God who justifies. *Who is he who condemns?* It is Christ who died, and furthermore is also risen, who is even at the right hand of God, who also makes intercession for us. *Who shall separate us from the love of Christ?* (Romans 8:31-35, emphasis added)

Paul asked five questions that are intended to lead the reader to the conclusion that God is not a passive Being who exists at a distance, watching us as we struggle through life on our own. He is a God who fought for us unto death on a cross, and who now fights for us in intercession, loving us in our shame, guilt, fear and condemnation, and bringing us into the liberty purchased for us on the cross. His love is perfect.

Paul concluded chapter eight of Romans with one of the most remarkable statements in all the Word of God:

> *For I am persuaded* that neither death nor life, nor angels nor principalities nor powers, nor things present nor things to come, nor height nor depth, nor any other created thing, shall be able to separate us from the love of God which is in Christ Jesus our Lord. (Romans 8:38-39, emphasis added)

God pursued Paul again and again, persuading him of His love and breaking down the arguments that waged war against this truth. God wore him down with the truth, set his heart free from fear, overwhelmed him with love, and brought him into the confidence of knowing that nothing—*nothing*—could get in the way of God's love for him.

The Church today needs to be persuaded of the reality of God's love for us, God's commitment to us and God's ability to help us. This persuasion won't happen overnight, but it can happen. I pray this generation will begin to cry out for it to happen. I pray that we will begin to recognize that the battle is waged in our hearts. As we declare war on the lies about God, the power of the lies and deception will be broken by the truth of God's Word. We must build our lives on the Word of God and allow the truth of it to usher us into the true knowledge of God.

CHAPTER

The Father's Answer: Proverbs 2

When I came to terms with just how lacking I was in the knowledge of God, I joined Job's friend, Elihu, in declaring, "Behold, God is great, and we do not know Him." When I was faced with the Scriptural, Biblical, *real* God, I realized I didn't know what I thought I knew, and I began to cry out for real knowledge. I said, as you may be saying even now, "I can't take it any more! How can my life be brought into a deeper and more intimate understanding of God? How can I find the knowledge of God?"

This is the best question we can ask. We must have poverty of spirit to ask this question—the realization that we can't achieve this knowledge on our own. There is a correlation between poverty of spirit and the knowledge of God: the Bible tells us that the poor in spirit, those who are hungry for true knowledge, will inherit the Kingdom of Heaven. The Lord wants the cry for the knowledge of God inside of us to grow and grow and grow until it consumes our thoughts. We have to want the knowledge of God more than anything. Only the hungry eat and only the thirsty drink.

The second chapter of Proverbs gives the answer to this cry.

As Mike Bickle wrote in the foreword, realizing that we need to find the knowledge of God can be a painful process. We have to give up everything and forsake dead forms of religion that deny the power of godliness and true knowledge. Before and after the wisdom of Proverbs 2:1-5 come the warnings of Proverbs 1 and the later part of Proverbs 2. The warnings are what give weight to the wisdom of this glorious passage.

"My People Are Destroyed for Lack of Knowledge"

Proverbs 1:20-33 depicts Wisdom (the knowledge of God personified) crying out in the streets and raising her voice in the open squares, saying, "How long will you naïve ones love your ignorance?" In essence, Wisdom was calling the people to get their heads out of the sand and wake up to the prophetic call of the hour, because if they didn't, they would perish. They could not live in the "ignorance is bliss" mentality any longer.

Verse 24 describes Wisdom when she saw that the people had refused and ignored her warnings. She declared to them that since they had disdained her counsel, she would laugh at them in the day of their calamity. This calamity includes personal seasons of destruction, but is ultimately prophesying about the end of the age and the destruction that will come upon the earth at that time. Even when the people cry out for Wisdom in those days, she will not answer. They will not be given the knowledge of God because they hated it in the past. They rejected the fear of the Lord; therefore, they shall eat of that which they sowed during the years of disdaining Wisdom's counsel. Wisdom then closes out Proverbs 1 as she declares the benefit of listening to her: "Whoever listens to me will dwell safely" (Proverbs 1:33).

We see the same thing in the days when Hosea cried out to the people of the nation of Israel to turn from their idolatry and immorality. They heard the call to the knowledge of God but refused it. They shrugged their shoulders and went on with business as usual, not believing that they would be judged. The Lord saw their refusal of Him and said, "My people are destroyed for lack of knowledge. Because you have rejected knowledge, I also will reject you from being priest for Me" (Hosea 4:6). God, in His kindness, cried out for His children to hear Him and turn their hearts toward Him, and they still refused. It was their refusal—not God's lack of concern—that made them vulnerable to every ploy of the evil one.

In a later portion of Proverbs 2, we are told that the purpose of pursuing wisdom, knowledge, discernment and understanding is to deliver us from immorality. Today's Church is being destroyed by literal immorality (pornography, fornication, adultery, emotional soul ties), as well as by the idols of permissible pleasures and of the false knowledge of God. Paul said in 2 Corinthians 2:11 that we should be aware of Satan's many schemes against us. Although this verse mainly talks about how forgiveness closes the door to bitterness or self-recrimination, we know that the enemy does constantly plot against us. We are being destroyed because of a naïve or unconcerned attitude regarding the power of the spirit of immorality. We must wake up to the seducing power of the spirit that is waging war against us. Being filled with the knowledge of God is the only safe way to live, as Solomon said:

> Understanding will keep you, to deliver you … from the immoral woman, from the seductress who flatters with her words, who forsakes the companion of her youth, and forgets the covenant of her God. For her house leads down to death, and her paths to the dead; none who go to her return, nor do they regain the paths of life. (Proverbs 2:11, 16-19)

Solomon should have paid attention to his own words. An immoral spirit turned his heart away from God at the end of his life, bringing judgment upon the kingdom of Israel.

Years before Solomon turned away from God, he passed these warnings on to his son. Solomon told him not to be ignorant of the warning signs of calamity and the power of immorality, but to seek after the knowledge of God with all his heart. If he did that, he could be sure God would answer him. Solomon clearly laid out the path to pursuing the knowledge of God in Proverbs 2:1-5.

"My Son"

> My son, *if* you receive my words, and treasure my commands within you, *so that* you incline your ear to wisdom, and apply your heart to understanding; yes, *if* you cry out for discernment, and lift up your voice for understanding, *if* you seek for her as silver, and search for her as for hidden treasure; *then* you will understand *the fear of the Lord*, and find *the knowledge of God*. (Proverbs 2:1-5, emphasis added)

There it is. It's not mysterious or difficult. The Lord is making it clear that if we do these three "ifs," we will understand the fear of the Lord and find the knowledge of God. For some of you, an arrow of revelation just struck your heart as you read this. You feel a relief that you don't have to turn the world upside down looking for what you desire—it's right there in Proverbs.

When the truth of this first struck me, I realized that, like the prodigal son, I had wasted a lot of time trying to find out and figure out what I was made for without success, when the answer was there all along. But I also felt courage arising in me, a courage I'd never had before. I set out to return to the Father's house and find the knowledge of God.

We have to go back to the Father. We have to encounter the Father who sees us in our brokenness and feels compassion for us—the Father who runs to meet us in the place of shame and vulnerability, who falls upon our necks and kisses us in welcome. The Father is longing for us to turn and hear the call to return to the knowledge of Him.

Before we take the next several chapters and examine the implications of each of the three "ifs" listed in Proverbs 2, let's consider the first phrase of this glorious passage: "My son." I have read, meditated upon, prayed and preached Proverbs 2:1-5 for the past five years. It wasn't until recently, however, that "My son" leaped off the page at me. This phrase is vital because it reveals the Father's heart for His children. I am convinced that the Father's cry is for us to follow Proverbs 2 into His heart. The Father desires that His children not be led away by the metaphorical immoral woman, which is the spirit of this age, so cunning, so deceptive, so ravenous in its nature. The Father wants us to have the lifelong occupation of seeking the knowledge of God, and He wants us to live every aspect of our lives from that position.

I'm finding the Father's heart growing in me as I minister to thousands of youth across America. Today's youth need more than a hip, charismatic preacher who tells lots of jokes and talks about being relevant. They need more than instructors. They need spiritual fathers and mothers who long for their wellbeing and who are committed to protecting them at all costs from those who seek to harm them. They need leaders and mentors who challenge them to have a vision for their lives, who call them into their destiny of knowing God.

Whether or not the youth of this nation know or acknowledge it, they need something real that will keep them from destruction in the days ahead. That something is the knowledge of God. It's time we cried out for the Spirit of the Father to come upon those who are in leadership over the youth of this nation. The youth need to be called away from wasting their lives on lesser things and called into lives of pursuing God.

The majority of us, even in the Church, are wasting our lives doing good things instead of the best thing: living in intimacy with our Father in His house. We do a thousand things in His name, but the true and living knowledge of God is absent in our experience. We get burned out and bored when we continue serving without truly knowing God, without relating to Him intimately and personally. We need something more than our ministries. We need to be filled with God.

In Luke 15, the prodigal son came to his senses and said, "I will arise and go to my father's house." We desperately need to come to our senses. We need to acknowledge and eliminate the wasteful areas of our lives that cause us to live without having a true heart encounter with God. As we take the beginning steps toward the true knowledge of God, we will find a Father who meets us even while we are still far from Him: "While he was still a great way off, the Father saw him and had compassion, and ran and fell on his neck and kissed him" (Luke 15:20). Our Father will reveal His heart and His commitment to us, and this revelation will mature us and bring us into the knowledge of God.

As we begin to grow in the knowledge of God and in our comprehension of His love for us, we will begin to understand the heart behind Proverbs 2. God is a Father who longs for us to know abundant, eternal life. He meets us in our most vulnerable and repentant place and elevates us to be with Him where He is. Jesus said that His Father, who gave all of His children (us) to His Son, is greater than all, and no one is able to snatch us out of His Father's hand (John 10:29). Jesus knew that His Father longed to be with His children. That was why He was sent to die—to restore the relationship between God and His children: "Holy Father, keep through Your name those whom you have given Me, that they may be one as We are" (John 17:11). Solomon exhorted his son to value the intimate knowledge of God above everything else:

> Wisdom is the principle thing; therefore get wisdom. And in all your getting, get understanding. Exalt her, and she will promote you; she will bring you honor, when you embrace her. She will place on your head an ornament of grace; a crown of glory she will deliver to you. (Proverbs 4:7)

"My son" is the heartbeat of Proverbs 2. It reveals the emotions of a Father who longs to protect his son from evil and to lay out the simple paths of seeking and finding God. Proverbs 2 gives us the way to see and follow God with all of our hearts.

We need long-term vision more than ever in this age. If we lack vision, we will not survive (Hosea 4:6). If we don't know where we are going, we will easily get off track; we will give in and give way when something else distracts us. So many people do not have direction or focus. We might get excited about a conference or a verse for a little bit, but then we go back to life as it was. We are so fixed on the "right now," on living only for today, that we've lost sight of the necessity of having long-term goals. This is devastating not only to us, but to the generations to follow. We need a long-term vision of growing in the knowledge of God. We need to embrace the lifelong journey of finding Him.

The Word teaches us that the way to avoid the temporal pleasures of this age is to seek the glory of the fear of the Lord and the knowledge of God. Through His Word, God reveals Himself to His sons and daughters and gives them a life vision for pursuing Him. He is preparing a generation of people who will not be moved from their vision of eternity.

Vision for Pursuing the Proverbs 2 Path

When Jeremiah told his generation to seek God, he said not to look for new paths. "Stand in the ways and see, and ask for the old paths, where the good way is, and walk in it; then you will find rest for your souls" (Jeremiah 6:16). These are the old, the sure, the tried and true ways of finding God. These are beautiful boundary lines that keep us from being ensnared by the enemy. These are the pathways to God and His heart.

There are three distinct "ifs" laid out in Proverbs 2:1-5. Each of these "ifs" is an ocean of truth and wisdom that will take us eternity to search out. Solomon made it clear that if we begin to give ourselves practically to these "ifs," we will grow in the knowledge of God. We don't have to walk in perfection in every area of our lives before we can reach the "then" reality of gaining the fear of the Lord and the knowledge of God. We don't gain this reality after a few days of studying, either. Revelation of the knowledge of God is an ongoing process. God designed it that way. As we begin to implement these realities in our everyday lives, our experience and understanding in the fear of the Lord and the knowledge of God will grow bit by bit over time. It will increase more in some seasons than others, but it will steadily increase. In the times when the journey seems boring and monotonous, we must hold fast to the promise of God's Word and know that, whether we feel it or not, we are being changed every day. The process takes time, diligence and focus, but we *will* know God.

The Lord doesn't change and He always keeps His promises. The long-term, on-going nature of seeking God transforms our character—it works patience, perseverance and humility in us, making us able to receive and fiercely protect what God gives us of Himself. This process is not like a fast food drive-through where we order our knowledge of God value meal, pick it up at the window and gulp it down as we drive away. The pursuit of the Holy takes us through the paths of prayer, fasting, diligence and perseverance, that we may reach the great prize of knowing God.

In Peter's second epistle, he described the heart values that must be working in us as we seek after the knowledge of God.

> But also for this very reason, giving all diligence, add to your faith virtue, to virtue knowledge, to knowledge self-control, to self-control perseverance, to perseverance godliness, to godliness brotherly kindness, and to brotherly kindness love. *For if these things are yours and abound, you will be neither barren nor unfruitful in the knowledge of our Lord Jesus Christ.* For he who lacks these things is shortsighted, even to blindness, and has forgotten that he was cleansed from his old sins. Therefore, brethren, be even more diligent to make your call and election sure, for if you do these things you will never stumble. (1 Peter 1:5-10, emphasis added)

These virtues are increased in our souls as we embrace the values of Proverbs 2. It's all about vision. Peter stated that if we are not pursuing these values, we lack vision and can end up spiritually blind.

The scary thing is that many people start on this journey in their teens or early twenties, but when a few circumstances or disappointments come their way, their diligence and vision for the knowledge of God begins to wane. They find that the virtues that once flowed are not flowing anymore. Then bitterness creeps in and corrupts their inner life.

We must discipline ourselves to diligently pursue the values laid out in Proverbs 2, no matter what circumstances we must face. They are simple—but not easy—realities. It can be difficult for us to enter into and remain committed to pursuing them because of all of the distractions that surround us. This way of life is available to all. But this path of intimacy with God truly is a narrow one, and few choose to take it.

The Father is looking for and longing for those who don't just choose the path of knowledge for a few seasons. He is longing for a whole generation to start this journey and commit to it for the rest of their lives. If we want to be part of that generation, we must press forward like Paul, reaching forward for the prize of knowing God. Pressing forward means being drastic. It means sacrificing lesser, immediate pleasures in place of greater, eternal pleasures. It means risking that we will be misunderstood by everyone around us. It means following the leading of the Holy Spirit when it makes no sense to our natural minds. Pressing forward means dying to ourselves utterly. We must move past the latest craze, the latest catch phrase and the latest church management model. Instead, we must put our hands to the plow and our eyes toward the goal, committing to the path we've chosen with unwavering hearts.

Most of our heroes in the Bible understood how to persevere in the knowledge of God. They lived their entire lives in obscurity so they could be entrusted with something powerful in their later years. Look at Daniel. This man spent seventy years praying to God three times a day. He remained faithful to God in a strange land and did not defile himself with the king's delicacies or the Babylonian culture, though doing so would have made his life more

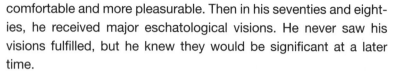
comfortable and more pleasurable. Then in his seventies and eight-
ies, he received major eschatological visions. He never saw his
visions fulfilled, but he knew they would be significant at a later
time.

Look at Anna and Simeon. These two people spent their whole
lives in the temple serving God with fasting and prayer, waiting for
the Messiah to come. They spent all of those years being ridiculed
and misunderstood, but when that Child came into the Temple, they
were the ones who recognized Him and met Him there. They met
the Son of God in the flesh, the Messiah whom the prophets had
foretold. That was surely worth the ridicule they must have endured
during their long years of waiting.

Look at Noah, at Moses, at John the Baptist. All of these people
lived lives of faithfulness in the midst of people who did not understand them, who must have mocked and scorned them. They toiled
day after day after day in their God-given mission. They feared God
and not man so that they could be counted as His friend. They had an
eternal perspective, a vision that surpassed their existence on earth.

That kind of eternal vision is what we must take hold of. The
call to the knowledge of God and the way to pursue it laid out in
Proverbs 2 are not new ideas. It is the way that God prescribed for
our forefathers and for us. We won't stumble upon the knowledge
of God if we aren't even looking for it in the first place. We have to
diligently pursue and seek it.

With all this talk of unwavering commitment, sacrifice and perseverance, many of you are wondering if you've got what it takes.
Just so you know, you don't. But God does. We are not alone in this
journey. God is with us and He is more committed to us coming to
know Him than we are. Psalm 63:8 reflects David's awareness of
who kept him going after God: "My soul follows close behind You;
Your right hand upholds me" (emphasis added). This whole journey
is about the One "who is able to do exceedingly abundantly above
all that we ask or think, according to the power that works in us"
(Ephesians 3:20), who is "able to keep [us] from stumbling, and to

present [us] faultless before the presence of His glory with exceeding joy" (Jude 24). This is God's heart for us and commitment to us as we seek after the true knowledge of Him.

Outline of Proverbs 2

Each one of the "ifs" in Proverbs 2 affects our journey into the knowledge of God. Again, it takes time for these "ifs" to become rooted in our heart, but as we persevere in pursuing the Holy, our diligence will pay off and our experience of God will increase.

There are four realities set forth in Proverbs 2 that lead us to the fear of the Lord and the knowledge of God:

- Receive my words and treasure my commands within you
- So that you incline your ear to wisdom and apply your heart to understanding
- Cry out for discernment and lift up your voice for understanding
- Seek Wisdom as silver and search for her as for hidden treasure

1. "If you receive my words and treasure my commands within you, so that you incline your ear to wisdom and apply your heart to understanding"

The first "if" speaks about how we posture ourselves before the Word of God and how we value the Word. The Word of God contains the knowledge of God and communicates it to our hearts. If we receive and treasure the Word, the Word will transform us. The Lord is raising up a generation of people who will delight in His Word, love His Word and arrange their lives so that the Word is living and alive inside them.

2. "So that you incline your ear to wisdom and apply your heart to understanding"

Through encounter with the Word of God, we are transformed and brought into agreement with who God is and how He leads.

The inclining and applying speak of our practical obedience and of how the Word begins to remove everything that hinders our full agreement with God. The Word moves into the core of our beings and wages war on everything that is against God.

3. "If you cry out for discernment and lift up your voice for understanding"

Crying out and lifting up our voice for the knowledge of God is mandatory as we move forward in the path. The first "if" and the "so that" speak of the receiving component of the journey. The second "if" describes the taking aspect, where we go after the knowledge of God with all that we have. This reality is characterized by spiritual hunger that will not be denied.

4. "If you seek her as silver and search for her as for hidden treasure"

We are treasure hunters, called to hunt for a treasure worth more than any of the treasures of this age. We won't accidentally find this treasure. We will find it only when we seek it with a wise heart. We can't go after the knowledge of God with uncertainty. We must understand that the vision is for life and that we must rearrange our lifestyles, our time, energy, finances and relationships now, today, to enable our life-long commitment to this pursuit. Doing so will dramatically affect our experience and growth in the knowledge of God.

We must begin to seriously consider how these phrases in Proverbs 2 will impact our lives and our experience in God. Over the next four chapters, we will follow the Proverbs 2 path into the Father's heart and into the knowledge of God.

CHAPTER

Receiving and Treasuring

The first reality set forth by Solomon has to do with the way we treat the Word of God: "If you receive my words and treasure my commands within you" (Proverbs 2:1). The receiving of the Word speaks of how we posture ourselves before the Word of God and the treasuring speaks of how we value God's commands.

Receiving: Encountering the Living Word

God expresses Himself through His living Word. Hans Urs Von Balthasar said so brilliantly in his book entitled *Prayer,* "God's word is Himself, His most vital, His innermost self" (p. 15). The knowledge or the life of God is communicated through the Word of God. Prayer is not meant to be a monologue. It is meant to be a dialogue that utilizes a specific language: God's language, His Word. Often we have to be quiet for a minute—shut down everything and sit and receive the Word.

This is the door, the medium, through which we converse with God and His life is opened up to us. If we do not understand the purpose of the Word, we will miss out on the life of God. Finding

God through His Word converts us into a better likeness and image of our Creator. Every word in the Bible is a divine door into the heart of God and a divine ladder that brings us into the spiritual realm to be with God where He is.

Words in general express the thoughts, desires, intents, purposes, emotions and will of the one who is speaking. The word manifests, declares and articulates that which was hidden. For example, I may look at my wife and feel deep love for her, but she isn't aware of it until I say, "I love you." It's the "I love you" that declares the hidden emotion. The Word of God is the "I love you" of God. It's the blueprint of His heart, of His mind, of His will. In particular, Jesus Christ is the living Word and expression of God, but it's through the written Word, the Bible, that we encounter Jesus. Jesus told the disciples, "The words that I speak to you are spirit, and they are life" (John 6:63). His words communicated the DNA of God. These words are alive with God's agenda.

We usually read the Bible like we do a good novel, magazine article, or historical account, and our common confession is usually, "I don't understand it. It's boring. It's weird." But when we approach the Bible with the right heart, our spirit is opened up to the realm of the Spirit. The Bible leads us into the depths of God, His heart, His nature, His character and His ways. The Bible is not an ordinary book, and should not be approached as such. This Book has to be approached differently—with awe, reverence and fascination, with the understanding that we tread on holy ground the moment our eyes look upon the words in this Book.

Instead of reading God's Word casually or disconnectedly, I come to it with humility and expectation. I make a point to be intentional and engaged. And I acknowledge that Jesus is calling me to know Him as much today as He did thousands of years ago when the Word was spoken. Luke 10:39-42 tells of how Jesus went to the town of Bethany to visit his friends, Mary, Martha and Lazarus. Martha became annoyed with Mary because Martha was doing all the work to serve Jesus, while Mary just sat at His feet, listening to

His words. Martha said to Jesus, "Lord, do You not care that my sister has left me to serve alone? Therefore tell her to help me." Remember Jesus' response? "Martha, Martha, you are worried and troubled about many things. But one thing is needed, and Mary has chosen that good part, which will not be taken away from her."

Jesus wasn't saying that service isn't necessary or good or important. But He was saying that there is something more important: sitting before Jesus and listening to Him. That is the way to intimacy. We, like Mary, must come to Jesus with this heart posture. He pours His life into those who sit and listen. His words breathe life into our bodies and souls, making us living, breathing, spiritual beings.

I sometimes wake up in the morning and come before God feeling dry and crusty on the inside. As I sit before Him, my eyes on His Word, I picture God breathing His breath into Adam while he was still a lifeless clay formation. The breath that brought life to Adam is the same breath that causes us to wake up and come alive in the Spirit. God breathes on us through His Word. Whether or not I feel it, this happens every time I receive the Word of God into my spirit.

The Purpose of the Word Is to Encounter Us

God's Word is eternal and unchanging. It instructs us and communicates truth to us today in the same way it spoke to each generation before us. The Bible contains so much more than stories for us to tell our kids at Sunday school. It's the divine door into the ways and wisdom of God Himself. As such, coming before the Word of God is a serious matter. Every time we come before the Word, the Word of God pierces us to the core. It brings down our arrogance and pride, but edifies our spirits and enlightens our minds. Most importantly, the Word of God ushers us into encounter with the living God. That is its purpose. If we don't receive the Word with that paradigm, if we don't expect to meet Jesus each time we open the Bible, we become dry and unaffected and bored. We will only know *about* God; we won't truly know Him.

John 5:35 describes Jesus speaking to a group, which included the Pharisees, about His forerunner, John the Baptist. He told them that although they had been willing for a while to go out into the wilderness to listen to John's message, it hadn't impacted them. The Pharisees had gone to the John the Baptist conference and not been moved by his message. When it came down to how they viewed the Word, they had not been willing to acknowledge or accept the Word's indictment of their unbelief.

A few verses later, Jesus laid the boom on them. He did the indicting when He spoke to them about how they treated the Word of God. Jesus didn't condemn them for searching the Scriptures; He condemned them for the attitude with which they did so. He told them to go hard after the Scriptures, but to do it with the understanding that the Scriptures would lead them to the Word made flesh, Jesus, who was standing in their presence at that moment:

> But you do not have His word abiding in you, because whom He sent, Him you do not believe. You search the Scriptures, for in them you think you have eternal life; and these are they which testify of Me. But you are not willing to come to Me that you may have life. I do not receive honor from men. But I know you, that you do not have the love of God in you. (John 5:38-42)

How could the people who knew the most about the Word of God be the ones who killed the Messiah? The Pharisees studied the Word as their occupation. They had it written on their foreheads, on their wrists, on their anklets (Deuteronomy 11:18, Matthew 23:5). They knew the Word inside out, but the Word did not know them. The Word wasn't living, moving, breathing inside of them. They didn't even recognize Jesus because they viewed the Word as an end in itself instead of the means to encountering the living God. If they had treated the Word rightly—as the way to encounter God—they would have responded to Jesus as Messiah in the same way that Simeon, Anna, John, and Mary of Bethany did.

If they had received the Word and let it abide in them, they would have recognized who Jesus was.

How different are many of our Church leaders today? Not very. We have thousands—yea, millions—of ministers and ministries that talk about the Word and preach the Word and quote the Word, but are not intimate with the Word. Few understand that it's about encounter with Jesus, that it's about intimacy—the Word abiding in us.

What does it mean to have the Word abiding in us? It's being intimate with the Word. What does being intimate with the Word mean? It means allowing it to wash over us and move us. It means meditating on the Word and pondering it and letting it sink deep into us. It means coming humbly and expectantly before the Word and waiting. It means clearing our mind of everything else and letting the Word fill us. It means allowing the Word to guide us to our destination: encounter with Christ.

I think of the words in the Bible collectively as an airplane that will transport me into the heart of God. Often I jokingly say, "John Flight 5:38 is taking off this morning at 7:00 a.m. into the heart of God." Each flight has a different departure city, but they all arrive in the same city every single time. Each flight is a journey to the spiritual realm. What if we began to come before the Word every day with that mentality?

I appreciate the popular method of reading through the Bible in 365 days, especially for people who need a starting point in reading God's Word. I can't help but feel, however, that this method contributes unwittingly to a performance-driven or homework assignment kind of mindset. Either we consider ourselves superior for having accomplished the task or we approach it as a chore we have to complete before we are allowed to have fun. Both mindsets cause us to be robbed of the gift, the privilege, of encountering Jesus. You can't cram for a relationship the way you cram for a test. Sure, you can memorize Scripture and quote it eloquently to others, but that's missing the whole point. The point is for us to actually take the Word into our spirits and have it written on our hearts. What does it really matter if you have Scripture written on your coffee mug, your calendar or your key chain if it's not written on your heart?

What if, rather than reading through the Bible in a year, we read one verse over and over for an entire year? I once spent six months reading and meditating on "Father, I desire" from John 17:24. I could not get over the fact that *desire* was at the heart of the cross. When God and His desire for me connected inside me, it was like nitrogen and glycerin. It was a spiritual explosion from which I still haven't recovered. Before that explosion, it was like God was a tiny, black-and-white television with one channel, but when the re-alization of what that verse meant hit me, bam! God became a one hundred-inch color television with a plasma screen and a thousand channels. God came alive to me, and I felt love and gratitude for Him like never before. Once I had received the Word like that, I be-gan to enjoy God and His Word. I was fascinated by Him. I couldn't wait to open the Bible. I knew there was more and I wanted to find it. I felt the power and emotion of God and His Word as I read the Bible. God went from being a stoic, detached Being who silently watched human beings from far away, to being a Father who had emotions and feelings and who longed for, loved and desired me.

How to Receive the Word in a Practical Way

So how do we read the Bible differently? How do we set our-selves up, practically speaking, for encounters in the Word?

One of the practical ways to read the Bible is through meditation: deep study and dialogue with the living Word. People meditate on the Bible in different ways. I am not saying my way, the method I outline below, is the best way, but it has provided an effective and practical means for me to converse with and relate to God through His Word. I have meditated on the Word in this way for the last eight years. The Word has become the source of my strength, motivation, encourage-ment, and wisdom for all that I do in the Kingdom of God.

Most of us have had the experience of reading the Bible and having a verse or phrase leap off the page at us. Perhaps we've never understood or really thought much about the verse before, but when it jumps out at us, we get revelation about it. In other words, we suddenly understand its meaning. Through the verse, the Holy Spirit is, in essence, telling us to stop, to come see, hear and encounter the reality that is set forth in that verse or phrase. The Holy Spirit was sent to lead us into all truth (John 16:13), and He does this when we stop and begin to talk to Him about the phrase or verse He has highlighted to us.

When something in the Bible pops out at me, I pay attention to the thoughts and emotions it is producing in me. I take the phrase or verse and begin to ask the Holy Spirit questions. I ask for understanding of what is being set forth in the Word. I ask God to share with me His heart about that verse. I ask Him why it's in the Word and why it's leaping out at me at that time. There are hundreds of questions we can ask about one single verse or phrase. For instance, right now I'm in John 16:13, meditating on the last couple of phrases in that verse: "Whatever [the Holy Spirit] hears, He will speak; and He will tell you things to come." I have been coming back to this verse over and over for the last month, and I've begun to ask questions and pray prayers like, "What are you hearing? Holy Spirit, tell me what you're hearing. Tell me things to come."

After we ask our questions and pray, it's necessary for us to stop talking and simply commune with the Spirit over our questions and prayers. The Spirit inside of me has birthed the questions and prayers, so I listen and wait for Him to give me understanding. This waiting mode is not intended to be a let-your-mind-wander, think-about-what-you'll-have-for-dinner mode. It's important to stay engaged. I usually pray quietly in tongues or sit silently with my mind focused on the words of the verse or phrase. Sometimes I sing the verse or phrase, pray it aloud, write it or read it. I do all of these things, not in a regimented way, but as the Holy Spirit leads me. I find that, as I wait, the Spirit gives me personal revelation. He imparts truth to my spirit, transforming me and awakening understanding in me about the verse or phrase. The Holy Spirit's favorite means of transformation is the Word of God. Every time, the revelation I receive when I meditate on the Word of God changes my understanding of God and my relationship with Him.

David understood that happiness is attained as we marinate in and become saturated by the Word of God. As we soak in God's Word, we are brought into the knowledge of God. In Psalm 1, David described how those who meditate on the Word will be blessed:

> Blessed (*happy or to be envied*) is the man who walks not in the counsel of the ungodly ... but his delight is in the law of the Lord, and in His law *he meditates day and night.* He shall be like a *tree planted by the rivers of water*, that brings forth its fruit in its season, whose leaf also shall not wither; and *whatever he does shall prosper.* (Psalm 1:1-3, emphasis and parenthetical comment added)

Let's stop reading the Bible just so we can feel good about having done our daily reading. Let's begin to actually stop and meet with God during our quiet times. Let's ask God to encounter us. God promises that whoever meditates on His Word will bear fruit and prosper in everything. That's a massive promise—a promise that I believe will be fundamental to awakening the Church in this hour.

Another powerful means of reading the Bible and encountering Jesus involves contemplation and silence. Meditation is initiated by us by reading and praying through the Word, whereas contemplation is initiated by the Holy Spirit. Both are two sides of the same coin and both accomplish the same goal. To me, contemplation is when the Holy Spirit turns the tables on us. He captures us and draws us into Him, bringing us into a place of fellowship and communion with Him that is deeper than normal. In this place of communion, He reveals more of His beauty and majesty, more of His love. He penetrates our souls and hearts with truth.

Silence enhances times of contemplation. Nothing causes me to feel more separated and protected from the things of the world like silence. In silence, I find that the Word impacts my heart and mind and soul more profoundly and speaks to me more clearly. Dialogue with the Word is vital, but so is silence. When the eternal Word speaks to us, sometimes all we should do is listen. As Balthasar said, "Prayer is a conversation in which God's Word has the initiative and we, for the moment, can be nothing more than listeners" (*Prayer*, p. 15).

Valuing the Word

We've been considering how we posture our heart before the Word of God. Now let's look at how we value the Word. The two are similar in nature, but it is helpful to distinguish between them and look at them from slightly different angles.

One of the most common, if not the most common, secretly-held opinions in the Church today is that the Bible is boring. Most people do not delight in the Word of God. Most of us do not fellowship with the Word. And, certainly, most of us do not encounter Jesus in the Word. We center our sermons around Scripture, we include the Word in our public prayers, we quote Bible passages in our evangelistic outreach efforts, and we reference the Word when we give prophetic words. All those uses are right and good and worthy. But if we approach the Scriptures *only* for those purposes, our life in God will indeed be boring and dull. Why? Because we were made to be in relationship with God, to fellowship with Him. We cultivate intimacy with Him as we spend time meditating on and enjoying the Bible. It is how our souls communicate with Jesus Christ, the living Word.

The Bible is not boring—*we* are boring. We have been deluded into believing that true pleasure and fascination come in the form of loud, stimulating, immediately gratifying entertainment that we don't even really take part in. We just sit there and passively watch or listen. It's over as soon we turn off the TV, walk out of the theater, switch off the stereo, win the video game, or shut down the computer. This kind of entertainment doesn't engage our spirits or make us more alive.

The Bible is divine entertainment—real entertainment. It contains the life of God, the Creator of heaven and earth. And I guarantee that it will blow the mind of anyone who is willing to enter in. We must see the Word of God for what it really is: a place of delight and pleasure.

Do you delight in the Word of God? What does "delight" mean, anyway? Delight means to enjoy, to love, to take pleasure in and to value something highly. Job said, "I have treasured the words of His mouth more than my necessary food" (Job 23:12). Jesus said the same thing: "Man shall not live by bread alone, but by every word that proceeds from the mouth of God" (Matthew 4:4). God will raise up a prophetic generation by causing people to fall madly in love with His Word. A people will come forth who love the Word of God more than anything else—who treasure the Word and understand that God meant for us to enjoy it. His Word was given to be loved, adored, admired and experienced, all for the purpose of drawing us into God Himself.

All this is not to discount the fear of the Lord. We should never lose our awe at the eternal Word of God. Isaiah 66:2 speaks of trembling at the Word of God. The fear of the Lord is important and will be discussed in a later chapter, but first we must be taught how to delight in His law.

Psalm 119: Happy Holiness

Psalm 119 is one of my favorite chapters in the Bible. It is divided into twenty-two sections—one for each letter of the Hebrew alphabet. The Psalm is written by David, the king whom the Lord called "a man after [My] own heart" (1 Samuel 13:14). From beginning to end of this Psalm, David praises and prays about the power of the Word of God. Most of us skip this chapter because all of its 176 verses seem to say the same thing. But it is important because it shows us how to delight in the Word of God. If you fall in love with this chapter, you will fall in love with the rest of the Bible. Psalm 119 is all about happy holiness, which means being divinely entertained by the Word of God. Happy holiness means that we joyfully deny the lesser pleasures of this world in exchange for receiving the greatest pleasures of all: being loved and enjoyed by God and loving and enjoying Him in return. I call this Psalm the alphabet of divine love.

The Psalm begins, "Blessed *(to be envied, happy)* are the undefiled *(blameless)* in the way, who walk in the law of the Lord" (verse 1, parenthetical comments added). In Psalm 119, David is sharing with us the secret, life-long love affair he has with the Word of God. The Psalm calls the Word of God by many names: the law, the commandments, the ordinances, the precepts, the statutes, the word. To David, it was all the same. Each word of God was a divine kiss (an intimate communication) from the heart of God. David loved to gaze in wonder at the beauty of the Lord displayed in His Word. He rejoiced in the consummation of all perfection.

What do you do when no one is watching? What is your secret pleasure or preoccupation? David's was the Word of God. When no one was paying attention, David snuck away to read and delight in the Word. God's Word was his greatest delight and he must have written Psalm 119 as a tribute to his love for the Word.

- "I have rejoiced in the way of Your testimonies, as much as in all riches. I will meditate on Your precepts, and contemplate Your ways. I will delight myself in Your statutes; I will not forget your word." (Psalm 119:14-16)

- "Your testimonies also are my delight and my counselors." (verse 24)

- "Make me walk in the path of Your commandments, for I delight in it." (verse 35)

- "I will delight myself in Your commandments, which I love. My hands also I will lift up to Your commandments, which I love, and I will meditate on Your statutes." (verses 47-48)

- "The law of Your mouth is better to me than thousands of coins of gold and silver." (verse 72)

- "Unless your law had been my delight, I would then have perished in my affliction." (verse 92)

- "Oh, how I love your law! It is my meditation all the day." (verse 97)

- "How sweet are Your words to my taste, sweeter than honey to my mouth!" (verse 103)

- "Your testimonies I have taken as a heritage forever, for they are the rejoicing of my heart." (verse 111)

- "Your commandments are my delights." (verse 143)

- "I rejoice at Your word as one who finds great treasure." (verse 162)

- "My soul keeps your testimonies, and I love them exceedingly." (verse 167)

Addicted to Eternal Pleasures

The Word of God was David's delight, his pleasure, his satisfaction, his joy; it was where he feasted on the beauty of God. I love the vow David made to the Lord: "I will delight myself in your statutes, and I will not forget your word" (Psalm 119:16). Other people didn't understand David's passion; they persecuted, mistreated, slandered and betrayed him. But when people spoke against him, he hardly heard them. In Psalm 119:23, he wrote, "Princes also sit and speak against me, but your servant meditates on your statutes." David was lost in another realm, addicted to the Word of God.

When Jesus chose His twelve disciples, His mission was to addict these young guys to His presence and His words. He wanted them to be fascinated with eternal pleasures. John 6 describes many of Jesus' followers leaving Him, rejecting His teaching. Jesus turned to His disciples and asked if they wanted to leave Him too. Peter answered, "Lord, to whom shall we go? You have the words of eternal life" (John 6:68). Even if Peter had wanted to leave, he couldn't have. He had burned all his bridges and had become addicted to Jesus, the Word made flesh. He was wounded by love to the core of his being, and nothing but the Word could satisfy him.

Paul delighted in the exceeding greatness of God and could not get enough of the pleasure of God. In Philippians 3:8, Paul wrote that he valued the Word more than anything else in his life: "I also count all things loss for the excellence of the knowledge of Christ Jesus my Lord." Like David and Peter, once Paul had touched Jesus, everything else was like dung to him. These people were ruined for Jesus.

God is calling a bored, dulled generation back to real pleasure—divine, holy pleasure—which is found in the Word of God. We must access the life of God in the Word or we will continue to live far from His presence. The Word is stronger than envy, jealousy, immorality, ambition. The pleasure of the Word rejoices the soul and enlivens the senses. So many Christians are barely surviving on lesser pleasures when they could be living lives of holy fascination and encountering God Himself in His Word.

David wrote in Psalm 16:11, "In Your presence is fullness of joy; at Your right hand are pleasures forevermore." Have you ever seen anyone abundantly satisfied? I think of myself after I eat a massive steak. I'm lying back in a recliner with a toothpick hanging out of my mouth. I don't want to move or talk to anyone because I've just eaten the best steak of my life. The fullness of God's house is a million times more satisfying than that.

David declared that those who seek out the Word to delight in it "are abundantly satisfied with the fullness of Your house, and You give them drink from the river of Your pleasures" (Psalm 36:8). What does a river of pleasures look like? I picture it like the chocolate river in *Willy Wonka & the Chocolate Factory,* except beyond that—it's beyond our wildest imaginings. We know from Revelation 22 and Psalm 46:4 that it is a real river. It flows from the throne of God, making glad the city of God and eternally touching our senses and emotions. Jesus promised that those who believe in Him and ask for the water of life will be transformed and will never thirst again. We will experience rivers of living water flowing from the Holy Spirit into our innermost being.

In Chapter 6, we will discuss the purpose of learning to receive and delight in the Word. We must allow the Word to reign in us and remove everything that hinders us from knowing God.

Inclining and Applying

We are to receive and treasure the Word of God (Proverbs 2:1) for a purpose: "so that you may incline your ear to wisdom, and apply your heart to understanding" (Proverbs 2:2). One precedes the other. We must first receive God's Word—God Himself—before we can incline our ears to wisdom and apply our hearts to understanding. The key phrase in this segment is "so that." That phrase tells us how God prepares hearts to encounter the knowledge of Him.

Inclining: The Transforming Power of the Word

We incline our ears and apply our hearts by setting our hearts on 100 percent obedience to the work of the Word of God in us. By nature, we do not want to listen to God, even when we are aware of the delights the Word offers us. Nor do we want to apply our hearts to follow God's ways. We want all of the eternal pleasures without having to change. It takes a supernatural effort of the Holy Spirit to work in us what is well pleasing to Him.

The Word's intention is to transform us, to bring us into the light and into full agreement with who God is. This is the knowledge of

God. It's more than getting through our daily Scripture meditation or having what we consider a productive quiet time. To have the knowledge of God is to have the embodiment of Christ in us. His life is contained in His Word, and the ultimate purpose of God is to manifest His life in us. Through His Word, His life is infused into ours.

Jesus spoke of the transforming power of the Word: "You are already clean because of the word which I have spoken to you" (John 15:3). James commanded us, "Therefore lay aside all filthiness and overflow of wickedness, and receive with meekness the implanted word, which is able to save your souls" (James 1:21). When we behold through Scripture what God is like, how He feels, and what we look like to Him, we are changed. We are not transformed by our resolve or our dedication, but by the power of the Word abiding in us. We are saved and changed to the degree that we receive the implanted Word. We have a part in the process and God has His part. He won't do our part and we can't do His part.

Our job is to receive the Word through meditation, singing, praying, and setting our hearts to full obedience. In order to do our part effectively, we have to understand and have faith that the Word has the power to bring transformation:

> The law of the Lord is perfect, *converting the soul;* the testimony of the Lord is sure, *making wise the simple*; the statutes of the Lord are right, *rejoicing the heart;* the commandment of the Lord is pure, *enlightening the eyes*; the fear of the Lord is clean, *enduring forever*; the judgments of the Lord are true and righteous altogether. More to be desired are they than gold, yea, than much fine gold; sweeter than the honey and the honey comb. Moreover by them *your servant is warned,* and in keeping them there is *great reward.* (Psalm 19:7-10, emphasis added)

This conversion process is not a one-time event. It is a long process that is painful at times, but wholly worthwhile. As we persevere in coming and sitting before God, the Word works in our inner man and changes our souls from the inside out.

The Word of God has the power to allure us, to draw us into the heart of God. The experience will seem completely enjoyable at first. The Word of God tastes sweet to us as we begin to experience its pleasures, as we begin to grasp the magnitude of God's love. As we pursue the Word of God more and more, it begins to change us so that we will be more like Him. We feel pain as the Word begins to move on the inside of us, waging war on the areas of our hearts that are in rebellion against the truth of God, His ways and His leadership in our lives. The purpose of the sweetness in the Word is to strengthen us to endure the bitterness of the Word. Balthasar understood that we have to know what will happen when we incline ourselves.

> This, then, is how the word of God draws a man into the truth; it opens up to him a world of love in which he feels at ease, which he is bound to acknowledge to be utterly right and suitable, to be most desirable. If he desires to stay there, however, his heart will be swept and purged to its innermost core. (*Prayer*, p. 234)

Despite the pain we will endure, we must pursue the conversion of our souls if we are to fulfill our destiny of knowing God. If we are starving for the knowledge of God to transform us, we will be willing to stay the course no matter the cost. Only by inclining and receiving the Word of God can we encounter the Word and be changed. We will find inner resistance on the front end, but if we are faithful in pursuing Him, the power of the evil one will be broken in our lives. It's with this understanding that we move forward in our journey through Proverbs 2.

The Inner War

The powerful thing about the true knowledge of God is that it gets right into the core of our being. It changes us internally, bringing the reality and truth of God to our spirits. We each have inner strongholds built with lies against the knowledge of God. The Word uncovers our internal workings and thoughts of unbelief, our lusts and jealousies, our bitterness and greed and covetousness. The power of the truth enters us to break our internal agreement with lies and darkness. God sanctifies and sets us apart with His Word, which is truth (John 17:17).

As we journey into the knowledge of God, we will all encounter seasons of confrontation, when the Word and the sin inside of us collide. We find, as Paul did, that a war is raging inside of us:

> For the flesh lusts against (*wars against*) the Spirit, and the Spirit against the flesh; and these are contrary to one another, so that you do not do the things that you wish. (Galatians 5:17, parenthetical comment added)

> For I delight in the law of God according to the inward man. But I see another law in my members, warring against the law of my mind, and bringing me into captivity to the law of sin which is in my members. (Romans 7:22-23)

As we get a vision for and pursue the deeper things of God, we encounter resistance inside ourselves. The law of sin is at work in us, and it cannot be overpowered by our own strength. We can't just wish that it were gone. We are broken and sinful by nature. Our past experiences and our environments have affected us. In fact, many of us are so fractured and wounded, it's amazing we can get along with each other for more than a few hours.

Most people spend a lot of time and energy trying to fix all of the problems in their lives with only counseling and prayer. These are powerful tools that aid us in our journey, but they cannot replace the implanted Word of God working inside us. It seems that in most churches, we keep cutting off the bad but we don't take in the good. We break off depression, addictions and fears, but we don't fill ourselves up with the knowledge of God and the pursuit of the Holy. For a time, our problems are kept at bay by what we heard at a seminar or by the deliverance ministry we received. But unless the seminars and deliverance are accompanied by a radical pursuit of the knowledge of God, the problems will come right back. We can't just break off the hindrances and strongholds; we need to deal with the root system that is producing them. We have to rip out the bad root system and plant the good one—the one founded on the Word of God and the deep things of God.

Part of the problem is that we live in a society that expects quick fixes. We want what we want when we want it, and we don't like putting forth effort to get it. But using quick fixes is like putting a Band-Aid on a gaping wound. The Band-Aid covers the wound for a short time, but doesn't cure the problem. If we really want to be changed, we must deal with our problems more effectively, and that means committing to a long-term journey. The division of heart and the tearing down of strongholds are only cured one way: by the Word of God changing us on the inside and bringing us into union with God.

In his book entitled *The Collected Works of St. John of the Cross,* St. John said: "The purpose of the Word is to impart, infuse the life of God. Where a soul is not prepared for this, or has things in opposition to it, the Word comes as a fire and burns the soul" (p. 650). Dying to ourselves and being transformed are necessary purifications and preparations so the Word may abide fully in us. The power of the Word has to wear us down so that we may receive the truth in our inner man.

Inclining to the Word doesn't come easily for any of us. Paul said, "The natural man does not receive the things of the Spirit of God, for they are foolishness to him; nor can he know them, because they are spiritually discerned" (1 Corinthians 2:14). We have to fight against our sin nature and allow the Word to move inside of us. We have to choose over and over to go against the desires of our flesh and trust that our reward will be well worth the sacrifice. We have to want the knowledge of God more than we want to keep our strongholds and secret sins.

As we set our lives before the Word of God, we will always find delight and joy in the eternal Word who lives inside of us. But we will also become aware of the bitter war within our members. As the Word exposes many areas within us that are in direct opposition to the Word of God, we begin to learn the price of inclining to this Word.

Applying Our Hearts: The Word as Judgment and Salvation

At this point, we usually begin to doubt God and what He is doing in our lives. We know that our pain is caused by the Holy Spirit revealing and destroying the lies and secret sins inside of us. We know He takes messed-up human beings and makes us more like Him. But *why* does God want to make us more like Him? Why is this painful transformation necessary? What is happening? Jeremiah wondered the same thing: "Your words were found, and I ate them, and Your word was to me the joy and rejoicing of my heart … why is my pain perpetual and my wound incurable, which refuses to be healed?" (Jeremiah 15:16, 18).

God's reason is that He wants us to know Him, not in theory or thought, but for real. He wants union with us through the Word. God wants to make a home within us so that His Word—His Son—can fully abide in us and we can abide in Him. He wants to possess us fully. But our secret compromises and strongholds hinder this union, for the Holy One cannot abide in the same place with sin. Through contemplative and meditative prayer, God begins to remove the areas in our souls that are not fully submitted to Him, in order to make room for His dwelling place. He prepares our souls by judging them.

If we begin to understand what He is doing and why, we learn to embrace it, pain and all. We begin to apply our hearts in obedience.

> *For in contact with the purity of the word he will come to understand his own impurity*; he will burn with the desire to be rid of it all costs. Of his own free will he will plunge into the flame, that the fire may not only illuminate him but also

consume and enflame him ... the fire to which he exposes himself will not abate until it has penetrated his inmost being, provided that he yields to it and does not draw back. (*Prayer*, 225, emphasis added)

Receiving and treasuring the Word isn't enough, and we can't stop at inclining our ears to the Word. We have to go all the way and apply our heart, walking out obedience to the Word of God.

Obedience is the manifestation of the Word of God ruling in us. It's the place of true rest, of depending solely and wholly upon the Father. Jesus emphasized active obedience the night before His death:

- "If you love Me, keep My commandments." (John 14:15)

- "He who has My commandments and keeps them, it is he who loves Me. And he who loves Me will be loved by My Father, and I will love him and manifest Myself to him." (John 14:21)

- "If anyone loves Me, he will keep My word; and My Father will love him and We will come to him and make Our home with him. He who does not love Me does not keep My words; and the word which you hear is not Mine but the Father's who sent Me." (John 14:23-24)

- "If you keep My commandments, you will abide in My love, just as I have kept My Father's commandments and abide in His love." (John 15:10)

As we cooperate with the Word's judgment of us and obey God as He brings to light our sin, we must keep a right perspective: it's better to allow the Word to judge us now so we won't fear to be judged before the great white throne (Revelation 20:11-12). It's painful to give up the pleasure or comfort of sin and to let go of bitterness. It's difficult to face our sin, especially when it seems like something new is highlighted every time we open the Word. However, the pain of judgment is absolutely vital in our Proverbs 2 journey.

The seasons of transition and refining are valuable as well as necessary. God begins to add the fear of the Lord to our delight in the Word. He produces in us a godly trembling before the Word that in turn causes us to want to obey Him no matter what. Again, why? Because of the connection between obedience and love, love and obedience. "He who has My commandments and keeps them, it is he who loves Me. And he who loves Me will be loved by My Father, and I will love him and manifest Myself to him" (John 14:21).

Another reason for these seasons of judgment is that God will find His resting place in the ones who give their whole lives in obedience to the power of the Word:

> Heaven is My throne, and earth is My footstool. *Where is the house that you will build for Me?* And where is the *place of My rest?* For all those things My hands have made, and all those things exist … but on this one will I look *(the gaze of heaven)*: on him who is poor and of a contrite spirit, and *who trembles (responds in obedience) at My word.* (Isaiah 66:1-2, emphasis and parenthetical comments added)

"Contrite" literally means "lame." It means that something within has been broken and wounded in a good way. People who have contrite spirits no longer put their confidence in the flesh; they are wholly dependent upon the Lord for everything. God is searching for those who are obedient, poor and contrite, and who tremble at His Word.

A Rest for the People of God: Hebrews 4

God wants a resting place for Himself. He is preparing human hearts to be in agreement with Him, to manifest the life of Christ in every thought, word and deed. In addition to preparing us to be His resting place, God is preparing our hearts to enter into a place of rest. Hebrews 4 says the rest for the people of God is found in Christ Himself.

> *There remains therefore a rest for the people of God.* For he who has entered His rest has himself also *ceased from His*

works as God did from His. *Let us therefore be diligent* to enter that rest, lest anyone fall according to the same example of disobedience. (Hebrews 4:8-11, emphasis added)

We will not fully enter into this rest until the age to come. However, a sizable portion of this rest is available to anyone who presses through inner and outer opposition and distractions. This ceasing from works doesn't mean we don't do anything. It means that we trust and obey God. In all that we do, we rest in Him even as we labor with Him. It means we allow Christ to live His life in us and we become totally His. We are not our own anymore. "For as many as are led by the Spirit of God, these are sons of God" (Romans 8:14).

The writer of Hebrews was not simply giving us hope that we can rest in God; he was telling us that, in order to do so, we must take action. He seems to cry out, "Let us be diligent to enter this rest." We must make a deliberate, focused effort to enter into this rest—the rest of full absorption into God and He into us.

How are we brought forth into this rest? We know by now that we can't enter this dwelling place without help. Hebrews 4:12 reminds us that our escort into this rest is the Word of God, who is a Man, our High Priest.

For the word of God is *living and active, sharper than any two-edged sword, piercing* even to *the division of soul and spirit,* and of joints and marrow, and is a *discerner of the thoughts and intents of the heart.* And there is *no creature hidden from His sight, but all things are naked and open to the eyes of Him* to whom we must give account. (Hebrews 4:12-13)

Let's not forget that we're dealing with the living Word. We can't just read the Bible when we feel like it. The Word is not passive. This Man—Jesus—is jealous for us to know Him. His love is a jealous love. He aggressively moves us into the rest of God. He sees, He hears, He knows, He feels and He *acts*. He is the two-edged sword of grace and truth, precise in His ability to find our rebellious areas. He pierces us to reveal how we are pulled between sin and holiness. All things are laid bare before the omniscient Judge.

We will experience different seasons and characteristics of the Word as we journey further into the knowledge of God. Depending on the season, the Word will be like cleansing water, burning fire, a powerful hammer, or the Hebrews 4 sword. As we incline our hearts to the Word through all seasons and apply it in our lives, we will come to know and understand the true rest of Christ. This rest frees us from our slavery to sin. We realize how little strength we have on our own, but how much strength God has and how willing He is to exert it on our behalf as we pursue Him wholeheartedly. When the rest of Christ illuminates our poverty of spirit, it produces a crying out for more of Him. In the next chapter, we will look at hunger.

7

Crying Out and Lifting Our Voices

In this chapter, we will consider the second "if" highlighted in Proverbs 2: "if you cry out for discernment, and lift up your voice for understanding." The first "if" was more passive in its receiving nature, but the second "if" is an aggressive laying hold of God for the deep things of His heart.

Crying Out

In the first "if," we are called to silence. In the second "if," we are commanded to cry out and lift up our voices. When God's people cry out to Him, that does something to His heart—it stirs something in the heart of God.

I believe voices are important to God. Psalm 47:5 says, "Shout to God with the voice of triumph … God has gone up with a shout." The entire Book of Revelation is about angels, elders and voices shouting with loud voices. The Second Coming of Jesus will be accompanied by a shout.

Hundreds of times throughout the Psalms, David cried out to God and called the people to cry out. One of my favorite Davidic cries is in Psalm 18:

> In my distress I called upon the Lord, and cried out to my
> God; He heard my voice from His temple, and my cry came
> before Him, even to his ears. Then the earth shook and
> trembled; the foundations of the hills also quaked and were
> shaken. (Psalm 18:6-7)

Solomon, remembering the lifestyle of his father, told his son
that the way into the knowledge of God was crying out to Him. God
isn't after literal volume, though this reality does include it. He is listening for a cry from the depths of our souls for more of Him. Once
we have given up on anyone else answering our cry to be filled, we
look to God alone to answer us, and that produces the cry of true
hunger. Hunger is the currency of heaven.

We receive salvation freely; it is a free gift given to us based
solely on Jesus' work at Calvary and we can never earn it. However,
through spiritual hunger we receive the deeper things of the Kingdom. I'm not saying that we earn intimacy with God, but receiving the deep knowledge of Him requires a certain heart posture.
Building a relationship always takes time and effort; it requires both
giving and receiving. We are worthy of His love simply because
He created us. He has loved us from before the foundation of the
world. But, just as in any relationship, we have to show ourselves
trustworthy with the deepest things of God's heart. The way we do
that is by demonstrating that we are hungry for the Word above all
else. John G. Lake spoke on hunger in *John G. Lake: The Complete
Collection of His Life Teachings*:

> God's purposes come to pass when your heart and mine gets
> the real God cry, and the real God prayer comes into our spirit
> and the real God yearning gets [into] our nature. Something
> is going to happen then … It becomes … the supreme desire
> of your soul, the paramount issue—all the powers and ener-
> gies of your spirit, of your soul, and of your body are reaching
> out and crying to God for the answer. It is going to come, it is

going to come, it is going to come. (p. 453-454)

Have you ever been really hungry for God? Have you ever seen hungry people? Hunger makes a savage out of us. Hunger makes us unreasonable. It makes us dangerous. It makes us miserable, yet completely focused and determined. Jesus said that people who are hungry should be envied above all, because their cry will be answered. Their hunger will be satisfied.

"Blessed Are Those Who Hunger"

I want to look at three of the seven glorious beatitudes Jesus gave in His first public message. These beatitudes contain the value system of heaven.

> Blessed are the poor in spirit, for theirs is the kingdom of heaven. Blessed are those who mourn, for they shall be comforted ... Blessed are those who hunger and thirst for righteousness, for they shall be filled. (Matthew 5:3-4, 6)

The world equates happiness with wealth, contentment and fullness, and would have us believe that the happiest people are the richest, most contented, best-educated people. In contrast, Jesus said that the truly happy people are those who are poor, mournful and hungry. He was making a clear statement that happiness is based on hunger and emptiness.

Being poor in spirit means that we understand we have nothing of value in and of ourselves. Without God's help, we are utterly unable to do anything to improve, help, change or save ourselves. We have nothing of value to offer God except that which He has given us. David's realization of this comes through in Psalm 16:2. He wrote, "My goodness is nothing apart from You." Our only hope is in God. As Jesus stated, "Without Me you can do nothing" (John 15:5). Poverty of spirit really is a gift from God, because from this place of poverty, the Kingdom of heaven is opened wide to us.

Mourning involves grieving over our poverty of spirit—our lack, our barrenness and our bankruptcy. I experienced the mourning spirit recently while preaching in front of a thousand young adults. I began my message by introducing a certain passage in the Bible. As soon as I looked down at the passage I was about to teach, I was overcome by my utter lack of true knowledge and revelation concerning the subject. I felt grief over my ignorant theories and over the lack of the true knowledge of God in the land. I cried for the full hour I was up on that platform. I'd never felt so vulnerable in my life.

After we recognize our poverty of spirit and after we mourn over it, being hungry is the next step. When we realize that we have nothing on our own and never will, we begin to hunger. We long to be filled. We begin to lift up our voices and cry out to God for the deep things of His heart. We begin to ask God to fill us with Him, because we now understand that we can never be filled by anything else.

God does things for hungry people that He does not do for others. I want to look at several examples in the Gospels that illustrate hunger. Remember, each biblical account is in the Bible for a reason other than providing Bible Baseball questions for Sunday school. They are doorways into the heart of God. I'm not saying we shouldn't educate our children about the stories in Bible. I am saying that as we do, we should instill in them an awareness of the weightiness, the glory and the magnificence of every word in the Bible. Let's remember that the Word was made flesh and was sent to make known what the Father is like. Jesus' interactions with people in the following accounts provide the perfect illustration of how God relates to hungry people.

The people in these stories were desperate. They were poor, they were in mourning, and they were starving for God. They did not have a Plan B when they came to Jesus. They were truly hungry.

Hunger in the Gospels: The Canaanite Woman

In Matthew, we read the account of a Gentile woman who came to Jesus and asked Him to heal her daughter.

And behold, a woman of Canaan came from that region and *cried out* to Him, saying, "Have mercy on me, O Lord, Son of David! My daughter is severely demon-possessed." But he answered her not a word. (*First test*) And His disciples came and urged Him, saying, "Send her away, for *she cries out* after us." But He answered and said, "I was not sent except to the lost sheep of Israel." (*Second test*) Then she *came and worshipped Him, saying, "Help me!"* But He answered and said, "It is not good to take the children's bread and give it to the little dogs." (*Third test, plus an insult*) And she said, "Yes, Lord, yet even the little dogs eat the crumbs which fall from their master's table." Then Jesus answered and said to her, "O woman, great is your faith! Let it be to you as you desire." And her daughter was healed from that very hour. (Matthew 15:22-28, emphasis and parenthetical comments added)

I weep at the enormity of this woman's poverty of spirit and at the desperation she displayed. She cried out to Jesus and to the disciples continually. Three separate times she pressed Jesus for a miracle. Even when the door seemed shut, she continued to knock and ask for a breakthrough.

Jesus tested her hunger and her persistence by causing her to ask again and again. First He ignored her. Next He told her that He was sent to the Jews, not to the Gentiles. Finally, He told her that it wasn't good to take the portion that God had set aside for Israel and feed it to the dogs. Jews often called Gentiles "dogs"; it was a demeaning insult. Yet she was not offended—she even agreed with Him. And she kept asking. Her agreement and complete poverty showed her faith. Jesus wasn't being mean; He was verifying her hunger. Like I said, God does things for those who are hungry that He doesn't do for those who are not.

Hunger in the Gospels: The Woman with the Flow of Blood

The next story is about a woman who could not stop bleeding:

> Now a certain woman had a flow of blood for twelve years, and had suffered many things from many physicians. *She had spent all that she had* and was no better, but rather grew worse. When she heard about Jesus, she came behind Him in the crowd and touched His garment. For she said, "If only I may touch His clothes, I shall be made well." Immediately the fountain of her blood was dried up, and she felt in her body that she was healed of the affliction. And Jesus, immediately knowing in Himself that power had gone out of Him, turned around in the crowd and said, *"Who touched My clothes?"* But His disciples said to Him, "You see the multitude thronging You, and You say, 'Who touched Me?'" And He looked around to see her who had done this thing. But the woman, fearing and trembling, knowing what had happened to her, came and fell down before Him and told Him the whole truth. And He said to her, "Daughter, your faith has made you well. Go in peace, and be healed of your affliction." (Mark 5:25-34, emphasis added)

Mark brilliantly gave his readers a small history of this woman's life: "She had spent all that she had." That powerful phrase invites us into her pain and her literal poverty. What had the days, months and years been like before she encountered Jesus? How deep had her poverty, mourning and hunger become by the time she grabbed Jesus' garment? Thousands of people had been pressing up against Jesus, yet He asked, "Who touched Me?" The hunger forged by her utter lack gave such authority and faith to her touch that Jesus felt it.

This story is a picture of the Church today. We have thousands of people coming around Jesus—going to church, singing the songs and reading the verses—but few who truly touch Him. What touches His heart and spurs Him to respond isn't louder volume at prayer meetings, or increased numbers of new members on the church roster, or catchy new songs and dances. Jesus responds to one thing: hunger.

Hunger in the Gospels: Blind Bartimaeus

Last, we are going to look at one of my favorite stories, the story of blind Bartimaeus.

> Now they came to Jericho. As He went out of Jericho with His disciples and a great multitude, blind Bartimaeus, the son of Timaeus, sat by the road begging. And when he heard that it was Jesus of Nazareth, *he began to cry out* and say, "Jesus, Son of David, have mercy on me!" Then *many warned him to be quiet; but he cried out all the more*, "Son of David, have mercy on me!" So *Jesus stood still* and commanded him to be called. Then they called the blind man saying to him, "Be of good cheer. Rise, He is calling you." And throwing aside his garment, he rose and came to Jesus. So Jesus answered and said to him, *"What do you want Me to do for you?"* The blind man said to Him, "Rabboni, that *I may receive my sight."* Then Jesus said to him, "Go your way; your faith has made you well." And immediately he received his sight and followed Jesus on the road. (Mark 10:46-52, emphasis added)

Jesus was thronged by thousands of people and couldn't have been expected to be able to hear much over the noise. Still, Bartimaeus was desperate enough to cry out. Those around him told him to be quiet, but encountering resistance only caused him to cry out more.

Jesus, the Son of God, stopped in His tracks when He heard the hunger in this man's voice. What Jesus said to this beggar has to be one of the most profound statements in the Bible: "What do you want Me to do for you?" In that moment, God became a beggar's servant, saying, "Here's a blank check. Fill it out; I'll give you anything you want." Bartimeaus' answer was as profound as

Jesus' question. And it is a prophetic reply for the hour of history in which we live: "Lord, that I may see!"

Oh, that the Church would be desperate enough to cry out, even in the face of opposition and discomfort; to cry out despite ridicule and accusation. We in the Church must come to terms with reality. We are blind, wretched and poor, but we don't know it. Jesus longs for us to realize the truth so that we will seek Him. He wants us to cry out in our poverty, in our mourning and in our hunger so that He can give us what we are seeking—gold refined in the fire (Revelation 3:17-18), which is the knowledge of God.

We must lift up our voices in a deep, desperate cry that ascends before the throne of God. The psalmist said, "Out of the depths I have cried to You, O Lord; Lord, hear my voice!" (Psalm 130:1) and "Deep calls unto deep" (Psalm 42:7).

Laying Hold of God: Spiritual Violence

In all of our crying out and lifting up our voices, we find out that our Father has a soft spot, so to speak. His soft spot responds to our poverty, our persistence, our hunger. Jesus told a story to illustrate persistence in prayer:

> And He said to them, "Which of you shall have a friend, and go to him at midnight and say to him, 'Friend, lend me three loaves; for a friend of mine has come to me on his journey, and I have nothing to set before him'; and he will answer from within and say, 'Do not trouble me; the door is now shut, and my children are with me in bed; I cannot rise and give to you'? I say to you, though he will not rise and give to him because he is his friend, yet because of his persistence he will rise and give him as many as he needs. (Luke 11:5-8)

The very next two verses are ones with which most of us are very familiar. Jesus continued:

> So I say to you, ask, and it will be given to you; seek,

and you will find; knock, and it will be opened to you. For everyone who asks receives, and he who seeks finds, and to him who knocks it will be opened. (Luke 11:9-10)

The friend described in verses 5-8 got up and gave bread to the man at the door, not because the man was his friend, but because the man was persistent. He steadfastly refused to give up and stop asking. The Father loves to give good things to His children (Matthew 7:9-11), but He wants us to ask and seek. He's not being stingy or manipulative. He wants us to ask and seek, because when we do so, we are communicating with Him. Communicating with Him causes us to intimately know Him, which is what God desires. Through the story of the friend and the bread, Jesus was showing us that sometimes God uses seemingly impossible situations to teach us how to consistently and persistently cry out. The Lord uses obstacles to produce godliness, perseverance, patience, and self-control in us. We learn how to ask for provision, not only for our current situation, but for every aspect of our life. We learn how to ask God to open up the house and give us as much bread as we need, as many times as we need it.

We live in a passive society, even in the Church. We tend to wait until "God's perfect timing" is revealed for the release of prophecies, healing, or other promises. Our wrong ideas of sovereignty keep us sitting around doing nothing. Isaiah said, "There is no one who calls on Your name, who stirs himself up to take hold of You" (Isaiah 64:7). We can have as much of God as we want. Those who cannot live without God, do not live without God; those who can live without Him, do. It's that simple. God is not complacent, apathetic, detached or unemotional. He longs for us to come after Him—because we want to, because we long to.

God honors and answers the asking, seeking and knocking described in Matthew 7:7 and in Luke 11:9, which are both really just rephrases of Proverbs 2:3. Each verse communicates the same thing: as we answer God's call to actively pursue Him, seeking to lay hold of Him and seeking the knowledge of God, He will give us what we desire.

Paul told Timothy, "This charge I commit to you, son Timothy, according to the prophecies previously made concerning you, that by them *you may wage the good warfare*" (1 Timothy 1:18, emphasis added). Paul was telling Timothy that prophecy invites us into an active participation through prayer and fasting. So many of us are sitting around with twenty-year-old prophecies, burned out and bitter because the Lord did not come like we thought He would or do what we thought He would do. What we don't understand is that the purpose of His promises is to draw us to Him in hunger. He wants us to reach for the knowledge of God.

Paul longed to know Jesus and to be found in Him. He was consumed with greater entrance into the knowledge of God in Christ:

> Not that I have already attained, or am already perfected; but *I press on*, that I may *lay hold* of that for which Christ Jesus has also laid hold of me. Brethren, I do not count myself to have apprehended; but one thing I do, forgetting those things which are behind and *reaching forward* to those things which are ahead: *I press* toward the goal for the prize of the upward call of God in Christ Jesus. (Philippians 3:12-14, emphasis added)

Matthew 11:12 records Jesus saying, "the kingdom of heaven suffers *(permits, allows)* violence, and the violent take it by force" (parenthetical comment added). God answers the cries of weak people who persistently lay hold of Him, who refuse to stop asking for breakthrough in their lives.

The powerful thing about crying out and lifting up our voices is the reality of "taking," as Jesus called it. In the first "if," we are told to receive the Word. In this "if," we are told to go after the Word. We are called to both receive and take—not one or the other, but both of them. The receiving fuels the taking. If our receiving ends with receiving, it hasn't accomplished its full purpose. Like God breathing into Adam's nostrils, receiving empowers us to stand and lay hold of the fullness of our destiny: the knowledge of God.

This taking is defined throughout Scripture. In Revelation 10, John saw an angel holding a book that contained God's plan for the End Times. John was told to go and take the book, to understand the knowledge within it:

> Then the voice which I heard from heaven spoke to me again and said, "Go, take the little book which is open in the hand of the angel who stands on the sea and on the earth." So I went to the angel and said to him, "Give me the little book." And he said to me, "Take and eat it; and it will make your stomach bitter, but it will be as sweet as honey in your mouth." Then I took the little book out of the angel's hand and ate it. (Revelation 10:8-10)

God, in essence, was saying, "If you want it, come and get it." If you want the knowledge of God, then put aside every weight and hindrance and reach for it (Hebrews 12:1). If you want the knowledge of God, then press in, take hold of it, and swim against the current of the spirit of this age. If you want it, shake yourself from the dust, put on your strength, and put on your beautiful garments (Isaiah 52:1-2). If you want it, cry out!

The Context of Spiritual Violence

Spiritual violence must be preceded by a revelation of the Father's heart, which we touched on in Chapter 4. In Luke 3, we read about when Jesus heard the Father say, "You are My beloved Son; in You I am well-pleased." From that revelation of the Father's heart for Him, Jesus was empowered to fast for forty days in the wilderness and to resist Satan. In Romans 8:15, Paul wrote, "[We] received the Spirit of adoption by whom we cry out, 'Abba, Father.'" The spirit of adoption is the spirit of prayer that unlocks our souls and shows us how to cry out freely to our Father in heaven. God's heart is moved when He sees His children seeking Him. When we understand the Father's heart and our value to Him as His sons and daughters, we are moved to violently lay hold of Him.

Paul defined the sons of God, which means both men and women, as those who are led by the Spirit (Romans 8:14). What does it mean to be led by the Spirit? It means that we are governed by and consumed with what God wants. Spiritual violence is having the freedom to do whatever God says and to throw ourselves into His arms.

Our Father wants to be pursued. He wants us to go after Him radically and to put aside our fears and restraints in order to do so. He knows we are going to backslide and make mistakes. He knows we are afraid of stumbling in our pursuit of Him. The only thing that is going to liberate us from fear is the revelation of the Father's absolute commitment to us. Perfect love casts out fear (1 John 4:18).

Paul encouraged the Roman church in spiritual violence. He didn't view God's love as something to think about only when there's some pleasant music playing in the background and everything is all right in our lives. He used the Father's committed love to prepare the Romans for future martyrdom:

> What then shall we say to these things? *If God is for us, who can be against us?* He who did not spare His own Son, but delivered Him up for us all, *how shall He not with Him also freely give us all things? Who shall bring a charge against God's elect?* It is God who justifies. *Who is He who condemns?* It is Christ who died, and furthermore is also risen, who is even at the right hand of God, who also *I am persuaded* makes intercession for us. *Who shall separate us from the love of Christ? ...* For I am persuaded that neither death nor life, nor angels nor principalities nor powers, nor things present nor things to come, nor height nor depth, nor any other created thing, shall be able to separate us from the love of God which is in Christ Jesus our Lord. (Romans 8:31-35, 38-39, emphasis added)

If we are to call our generation to spiritual violence, we must call them in the context of the revelation of the Father's resolute love for us. It's not about our commitment to God; it's about God's commitment to us. In Psalm 63:8, David wrote, "My soul follows close behind you; Your right hand upholds me." Unless we tap into this revelation—that God's hand strengthens us—we will quickly grow tired and faint in our pursuit of God. If we are to give ourselves to this for years, we need to drink deeply of God's commitment to us. That will keep us running our race with endurance for all our lives.

I love the "Now to Him's" of Scripture; they remind us that we are dependent upon the ability of God to work in us what is well pleasing to Him. In Ephesians 3:16-20, Paul prayed, "Now to Him who is able to do exceedingly abundantly above all we could ask or think." He prayed for the Ephesian believers, asking that Christ would live in their hearts and fill them with the fullness of God. Paul knew this church would never in a million years be able to pursue God in their own strength, so he instructed them to trust in God's ability, God's commitment and God's love for them. He emphasized the same thing to the Thessalonian church: "Now may the God of peace sanctify you completely ... that you would be preserved blameless at the coming of our Lord Jesus Christ. He who calls you is faithful, who will also do it" (1 Thessalonians 5:23). The apostle Jude reinforced this when he ended his epistle with the words "Now to Him who is able to keep you from stumbling, and to present you faultless before the presence of His glory with exceeding joy."

We have to root ourselves in God's faithfulness to His own name and to His own glory. We've been deceived into believing our God is a god who is worried and insecure most of the time because nothing he does really works. That is an outright lie. Even when we are faithless, God is faithful, because He cannot deny Himself.

I am praying that the Father will raise up a spiritually violent people. Let a cry arise all over the earth for the presence of the true, living God. I long for a spiritually violent generation that will press through everything to know God. In Chapter 8 we will look at the last "if" of Proverbs 2: how to lay hold of the knowledge of God.

Seeking and Searching

The last "if" in Proverbs 2 describes the lifestyle and wisdom of going after the knowledge of God: "If you seek her as silver and search for her as for hidden treasure." I have written throughout this book about the spirit of revelation. Paul also prayed for a spirit of wisdom. Revelation is seeing the desired goal; wisdom is choosing the best way to reach that goal.

The Spirit of Wisdom

The spirit of wisdom is an important part of the Proverbs 2 reality. Moses asked of God, "Teach us to number our days that we might gain a heart of wisdom" (Psalm 90:12). Meditation on and hunger for the Word need to be accompanied by wisdom—how to live toward that end. Wisdom teaches us to value and strive for the treasure of gaining living understanding of God, which is worth more than anything on earth. The treasure of the knowledge of God is eternal and cannot be destroyed (Matthew 6:20). These glorious riches are found in God and His Son. Paul spoke of "all riches of the full assurance of understanding, to the knowledge of the mystery of God, both of the Father and of Christ, in whom are *hidden all the treasures of wisdom and knowledge*" (Colossians 2:2, emphasis added).

Wisdom calls us to search out these riches like treasure hunters, and to give up everything else in the process:

> *The kingdom of heaven is like treasure hidden in a field,* which a man found and hid; and for joy over it he goes and sells all that he has and buys that field. Again, the kingdom of heaven is like a merchant seeking beautiful pearls, who, when he had found *one pearl of great price,* went and sold all that he had and bought it. (Matthew 13:44, emphasis added)

The fulfillment of the eternal meaning behind this passage was when Jesus came to earth and sold all that He had (as God, He gave up His perfect communion with the Godhead; as a man, He gave up His life) to buy the field (us). In the same spirit, we are now to sell (give up) all to purchase the eternal realities of knowing God.

The Kingdom of heaven and the knowledge of the King is our treasure. These riches are hidden to our natural understanding (1 Corinthians 2:14). In the same way that Jesus told Nicodemus that he had to be born again to enter into the Kingdom, we must change our paradigm so that we may enter into the Kingdom and have revelation of the King. We must count the cost of the treasure and be willing to give up everything to have it.

That's the power of the spirit of revelation. Once you get a little bit, you are ruined for anything else. I'm reminded of the principle that Jesus laid out and Matthew recorded: "For whoever has, to him more will be given, and he will have abundance; but whoever does not have, even what he has will be taken away from him" (verse 13:12). We want to be people who respond to the initial spirit of revelation with wisdom: radically sacrificing everything and embracing the Kingdom of heaven with all that is in us.

Voluntary Lovers

Why is the Kingdom of God a hidden treasure? Why does God hide Himself? The answer is in Proverbs 25:2: "It is the glory of God to conceal a matter, but the glory of kings is to search out a matter."

God hides Himself because He wants voluntary lovers who will do whatever it takes to acquire the treasures of God. Just as we don't want a passive, uninvolved God, God doesn't want passive, uninvolved followers. He wants people who are hungry for Him and who are desperate to be transformed by Him. In His wisdom, God uses the seeking and searching as the purifying fire that prepares us to receive what we find. Through our seeking and searching, we are changed into people who can steward and be trusted with the deep things of His heart.

In the last chapter, we looked at laying hold of God. Jesus taught His disciples that when they prayed, they would encounter a different side of God than the one they knew. They would encounter a God who would appear to resist them, who would provoke them to see what they would do when He did not answer. Would they give up? Would they be offended? Would they become angry and blame Him? Or would they press in and continue to ask Him for what was on their hearts? This is spiritual violence: continually seeking God's face, even when it seems He has turned His face away from us.

God doesn't always hide Himself, but this is one of the many ways He uses to draw us more deeply into His heart and into intimacy. One of my friends calls this the "intimacy conspiracy." God withdraws from us because He knows that His doing so will produce greater hunger in us. We will want to draw closer to Him all the more. We will do whatever it takes.

We are not alone in our search. The Father sent us the Holy Spirit to help us search out the knowledge of Him and to encourage us along the way. Think about it—we are called to a treasure hunt in which God has hidden the treasure in His Son, who dwells in us by the Spirit. The Kingdom of God is within us. The knowledge we have been searching for has been living inside of us all along.

Paul said, "Now we have received, not the spirit of the world, but the Spirit who is from God, that we might know the things that have been freely given to us by God" (1 Corinthians 2:12). Few of us are aware of what we possess in Christ and how much we mean to Him. God blessed us with every spiritual blessing in Christ, and we are hidden in Him (Ephesians 1:3, 1:18; Colossians 3:3). The moment we said yes to Jesus as Lord and Savior, God put within us His very own Spirit: "For [the Spirit] dwells with you and will be in you" (John 14:17). We become a new creation with new capacities and faculties. We are made for searching the deep places of God through the Holy Spirit. God is inviting us into voluntary, violent love.

Foolishness to the World

The call of wisdom is not only to spiritual violence; it is to weakness and complete dependence on God.

> But God has chosen the foolish things of the world to put to shame the wise, and God has chosen the weak things of the world to put to shame the things which are mighty; and the base things of the world and the things which are despised God has chosen, and the things which are not, to bring to nothing the things that are, that no flesh should glory in His presence. (1 Corinthians 1:27-29)

This passage makes clear that God has a controversy with the values, reasoning and lifestyles of the world, which are prevalent in our Western society—even in the Church. God declares emphatically, "I will destroy the wisdom of the wise and bring to nothing the understanding of the prudent" (1 Corinthians 1:19). He will shake the wisdom of man and expose its bankruptcy. He is bent on destroying the wisdom and understanding of this age, proving it incompetent in its ability to discern the knowledge of God and impotent in its power to affect change. It's all coming down to the wisdom of God versus the wisdom of man. "But let him who glories glory in this, that he understands and knows Me" (Jeremiah 9:24).

Right now, most believers in America are not building our lives on the knowledge of God. Instead, we are putting our confidence in how big our churches are, how large our bank accounts are, who we know and how gifted or anointed we are. We think these will help us spread the Gospel with more impact. We think our multimedia presentation or our newly renovated church building will win souls. We are secure in our own might, our own riches and our own wisdom. Yet that is contrary to how God has set up the Kingdom of heaven. Man chooses the strong, the rich and the powerful to run the world's business. God chooses the weak, the poor and the humble to run His Kingdom.

Please don't misunderstand me. I am not saying there is anything wrong with nice church buildings or having money or being gifted; all of those are of God and from God. I am saying it is wrong for us to place our confidence in those things rather than in God.

Jesus told Pontius Pilate, "My kingdom is not of this world. If My kingdom were of this world, My servants would fight so that I should not be delivered to the Jews [for crucifixion]; but now My kingdom is not from here" (John 18:36). Jesus was making it clear that His Kingdom is from another age and operates on a completely different system than that of this world. If His Kingdom had been worldly in nature, His followers would have gathered an army and defended Him. Instead, one of His friends betrayed Him, one denied Him three times, and all of them deserted Him. I don't think most potential leaders would buy Jesus' book on leadership training. He has a completely different definition of success.

The forerunners of the Bible operated under the Kingdom's values and definition of success. Noah preached repentance and judgment for more than a hundred years, just to see seven people get saved—and all of them were family members. Jeremiah prophesied the need for repentance for forty years to the nation of Israel, and nobody repented! What is this? How does this fit into our present mentality of what defines success? Based on the lives of the Biblical heroes, the only conclusion that we can reasonably draw is that our own wisdom is worthless. *God's Kingdom is not of this world.*

God put on flesh in the person of Jesus. He came in weakness and humility. Most of the people didn't even recognize who He was, even though He told them He was the Son of God and backed up His words with miracles. No one was following Jesus by the time His ministry came to an end; yet the apostle Paul wrote, "Christ crucified … [is] the power of God and the wisdom of God" (1 Corinthians 1:23-24). Who would have ever thought that a broken, bleeding man hanging in agony between two thieves was the greatest declaration of the wisdom of God? But God was never stronger than He was at Calvary. God was never wiser than He was at Calvary. After all, He told Paul, "My strength is made perfect in weakness" (2 Corinthians 12:9). The treasures of the knowledge of God are hidden in the foolishness of weakness. Only when we are weak and dependent on Him in every area in our lives will we find the knowledge of God.

The Fasted Lifestyle

Seeking and searching means that we heed the call to embrace weakness, foolishness, and insignificance for the purpose of seeing the Kingdom manifested. This was Jesus' call in the Sermon on the Mount—what we call the "fasted lifestyle." In living the fasted lifestyle, we embrace weakness in practical ways by giving up our own strength and resources. We do this by fasting food, energy, time and finances, and by fasting our words and even our reputation at times. God is glorified by our weakness, meekness, poverty of spirit, mourning, hunger, thirst, mercy, purity of heart, and silence in face of persecution—our powerlessness allows His strength to be displayed.

We give up our schedules, our food, our meetings, and our busyness. We choose not to speak against others and we choose not to defend ourselves. And in the silence that ensues, we hear the cry of our souls for reality. We see how barren we are without God. As we voluntarily embrace weakness, God reveals Himself to us. He promised in Hosea that He would bring Israel to the wilderness, the place of desolation and weakness; there He would give her vineyards, the things she longed for (Hosea 2:14-15). He will come to us in the wilderness—the Bible tells us the wilderness is the place of encounter, and the biblical accounts of people like Moses demonstrate how true that is. That is what our King is like and that is how He runs His kingdom. That is the path of wisdom.

Embracing the principles Jesus taught in the Sermon on the Mount—living what we at IHOP call "a Sermon on the Mount lifestyle"—will greatly enhance our journey into the knowledge of God. Giving generously to others out of our finances and forgiving our enemies don't earn us anything from God, but they prepare our spirits to receive the things of God, which He freely offers us. They put a bull's-eye on our chests, so to speak, that says, "Here we are, God; hit us with Your best shot. Hit us with the knowledge of God."

I want to look at two of the seven voluntary choices Jesus highlighted in the Sermon on the Mount, as well as the choice to pray in the Spirit. Choosing rightly in these three matters will help us tremendously in our search for the hidden things of God's heart. The discussion here of these three examples of voluntary weakness will be in no way comprehensive—an entire book could probably be written about each one. I just want to give you a taste of what we are called to in our search for the knowledge of God.

Fasting from Food

We can choose to fast food, which means we also fast energy. Fasting food seems strange at first. How would not eating help us become closer to God? How does being hungry increase our experience of God? God, in His infinite wisdom, decreed that if we pray instead of eating a hamburger, He will increase His presence and the Word will penetrate us more profoundly. It's based on voluntary weakness. If we sacrifice our strength for God, He will manifest His strength in us.

When people ask me how they can become hungry for God, I tell them there's only one way to get hungry: fast. Fasting food is one of the quickest and surest ways to be given the spirit of revelation. Nothing tenderizes and softens our hearts like fasting. Nothing makes us more sensitive to the Holy Spirit and to the Word of God like fasting. Fasting causes our spirit to dominate our flesh; it changes our whole internal structure, rewires us and transforms our minds. It causes the processes of revelation and transformation to speed up. Fasting food is truly a gift from God that expedites our journey into His heart. It is simply the way of God. It may not make sense to us, but God's ways are higher than our ways.

It is important for us to change the way we view the discipline of fasting. Most people see it as a duty and drudgery, something to be endured in order for God to be pleased with them. That couldn't be farther from God's intention. We are meant to see it as a gift from God, a precious gift that we can choose to open or not. Don't get me wrong. There are days when I have to constantly remind myself, "This is a gift from God." I'm watching the clock; I'm counting the minutes; I can't wait to finish my fast and go eat. But the majority of the time, my heart comes alive with love for God when I fast.

We choose to fast out of desire and hunger for God's presence, and God never fails us. And each time, our hunger increases and we become more and more ruined for anything less than Him. Jesus told His disciples that fasting was about being wounded with His presence, the presence of the Bridegroom: "Can the friend of the bridegroom mourn as long as the bridegroom is with them? But the days will come when the bridegroom will be taken away from them, and then they will fast" (Matthew 9:15).

Fasting plays a role in solidifying our identity as sons and daughters of God. At His baptism, Jesus heard His Father say of Him, "This is My beloved Son, in whom I am well pleased" (Matthew

3:17). After this affirmation, the Spirit led Jesus into the wilderness, where this declaration was tested by Satan. The forty-day fast that Jesus went through wasn't part of the test; it strengthened Him to endure temptation. When He emerged from the wilderness after the fast and the testing, He was ready to begin His work of revealing the Father to the earth.

Fasting doesn't earn us anything or make God notice us more. We don't have to make a name for ourselves and we don't have to get His attention. We already have His attention; we're already His beloved ones. He already notices and cares about every detail of our lives. What we are doing through fasting is opening ourselves up to Him and making ourselves more receptive to Him.

Fasting Our Time

Instead of spending our free time playing video games or using our lunch hour to run errands, we might choose to give that time to God. Practically speaking, fasting time involves the call to prayer.

Can you think of anything more foolish to the natural mind than sitting in a room, speaking words into the air to an invisible God, and trusting that He is hearing those words and changing things as a result? Let's say I'm here in Kansas City and I'm praying for Israel. I'm trusting that God is hearing my words and translating them into spiritual influence and power on people thousands of miles away. To us, it seems like an odd way to run a Kingdom. After all, couldn't God affect change on His own? Why does He need us?

The truth is this: God doesn't need us to be involved. He created the heavens and the earth without us. He created *us* without us. But He wants us to be involved in His Kingdom. He has chosen to have us partner with Him in His efforts because He enjoys our company. He wants to spend time with us.

I believe one of the most common reasons many people do not embrace personal or corporate prayer is because it doesn't make sense. It's not logical. It seems to us that we are much more productive, that our time is much better spent and that those around us are much better served when we are busy—when we're not praying, in other words. That's totally wrong. We actually do more to affect the earth when we pray than when we do anything else. Every ministry should be rooted in and powered by prayer; all of our service should be birthed in the place of prayer. If we really knew how powerful prayer is, we would prioritize our lives and operate our ministries and businesses very differently.

One of my friends tells a story about an old Chinese evangelist who spent decades in China winning thousands of souls for the Lord. He was crippled because of his age, unable to walk. Someone asked him, "How do you feel now that you are not able to go and evangelize China and win souls for Christ?" The man smiled and said, "You don't understand. When I pray on my bed in this little room, all of China shakes."

The reality is that God listens to our prayers. I teach a class entitled "The Eternal Glory of an Intercessor." I spend the semester emphasizing again and again that we were made for intimacy with God and have been given authority to intercede before His throne. What was lost in the garden at the Fall has been restored in Jesus, the eternal intercessor, as He joins hands with us in our poverty. Jesus wants to bring us up into heavenly places to partner with Him in intercession—intercession is His eternal priestly ministry. But we have to be willing to take the time to pray if we want to be "kings and priests to our God" (Revelation 5:10). The Lord will bring His Church into the fullness of her identity as a praying people in the days to come. He will call us to share His heart and partner with His purposes in the earth. His house will be called a house of prayer, and through prayer, the Church will help release God's Kingdom on earth in this age and in the age to come.

Most people don't realize how many hours are available to us in a week. We think we couldn't possibly find the time to spend extended amounts of time in prayer. When I speak to groups, I break down the 168 hours in a week. I allow 56 hours a week for sleep, 50 hours for work and/or school, 20 hours for getting ready and eating meals, and 15 for recreation (sports, entertainment, hobbies, etc.) That leaves almost thirty hours a week in our schedules! We could potentially spend four hours a day reading and studying the Bible, worshipping, praying, doing a devotional and interceding. What are we doing with our time?

Having time to relax and rest is important, but do we value our free time more than our time in prayer? How much of our time are we willing to give up? The seventy- or eighty-year lifespan that we have is our greatest commodity. The way we use it affects us now and it affects our future in the eternal Kingdom, because everything we do with our time communicates what we value the most. I'm convinced that, when we stand before God, we will give account for how we spent our time here on earth.

Praying in the Spirit

Praying in the spirit is also known as praying in tongues. This glorious mystery of God has been given to us as a gift. Unfortunately, this gift is hotly debated. Many people hold strong opinions about speaking in tongues, so it has taken a beating in doctrinal circles. I'm not here to defend the gift. I freely receive it and believe it is one of the great keys to unlocking the mysteries of God.

Someone once approached a friend of mine and asked, "Why do Christians have to speak in tongues?" My friend was shocked because it had never occurred to him that he *had* to speak in tongues; he had always considered the gift of tongues to be a great blessing and privilege. All he could manage to say was, "We don't *have* to speak in tongues; we *get* to speak in tongues."

God has hidden the eternal mysteries of Himself in babblings. Once again, it may not make sense to our natural minds, but it makes perfect sense in the supernatural realm. God chooses the foolish things of the world to confound the wisdom of the wise. Paul said, "He who speaks in a tongue does not speak to men but to God ... in the spirit he speaks mysteries" (1 Corinthians 14:2). He emphasized that interpretation of tongues was important in a public setting, but that speaking in tongues is a practice in which we can engage constantly. He must have done so, for he wrote, "I thank my God I speak with tongues more than you all" (1 Corinthians 14:18). I'm convinced that praying in the spirit was one of Paul's most essential doors into the spirit of revelation and transformation.

"He who speaks in a tongue edifies himself," Paul said in 1 Corinthians 14:3. Praying in tongues may sound strange, but we are actually building up our inner man by doing so. The Spirit searches the hidden things of God and makes them known to us. When we speak in tongues, we speak about who God is, what He feels, and what He's doing. Praying in tongues affects our hearts even if we don't know what we're saying. And it affects the spiritual realm, because the Holy Spirit is the one directing our prayers as He knows they need to be directed. Through this gift, we are equipped to hear and receive mysteries. We are being guided into all truth (John 16:13).

Praying in tongues seems like foolishness to outsiders. Many people in the Church don't believe in its validity or think it less valid than "normal" prayer. But I believe praying in the spirit is the way to prepare ourselves to receive the spirit of revelation. Over the last six years, I have tried to pray in tongues two to four hours a day. Giving up my time to speak in tongues has revolutionized my life and ushered me into God's heart.

We have explored all three of the "ifs" in Proverbs 2. The Lord has promised that as we embrace the realities set forth in these verses, we will find the fear of the Lord and the knowledge of God. We'll look at these two topics in the next chapter.

Understanding the Fear of the Lord

Proverbs 2:6: "Then you will understand the fear of the Lord and find the knowledge of God." We've considered the three glorious "ifs" of Proverbs 2. Now we will consider how they lead us into the reality of knowing Him.

The knowledge of God cannot and must not be treated lightly. This journey is not something we can put off for our entire lives and then rush through in a few days. We can't search for God if we still have wrong views and ideas about Him. We can't touch the eternity of God if we don't believe that what we do has eternal significance. And we can't understand the knowledge of God without understanding the fear of the Lord.

The Awareness of God

What exactly is the fear of the Lord? What does it mean to understand it? What does it meant to understand Him? To understand someone involves much more than mental comprehension. Mentally comprehending that someone is a person or that they exist does not mean you understand them. When we really understand someone, we understand their thoughts, emotions, and personality. We know about their past; we know about their future plans. We have discovered what motivates them, what delights them, what moves them. We know their likes and dislikes, their hopes and dreams. We know what makes them laugh and what makes them weep. And we are impacted by our awareness of them in their entirety. The same is true with God and our understanding of Him.

I would define the fear of the Lord as the awareness of God. As we begin to understand the fear of the Lord, we begin to feel the reality of God and who He is bear down upon us and stir our hearts. We begin to become aware of Him in His entirety.

You and I live under the watchful gaze of Almighty God. It is a loving gaze, but a searching one. Nothing we do is hidden from His sight. He sees all, He knows all, and He tests our hearts. Understanding this produces a godly fear of the Lord in us. Jesus sought to awaken this fear of the Lord in His listeners when He preached the Sermon on the Mount, where He spoke about the "God who sees in secret" several times (Matthew 6). Every second of every minute of every hour of every day, whether spent in the secret place or in public, matters to God. In God's sight, there is no difference between what we do at home when we're all alone and what we do in front of people.

The fear of the Lord comes from the awareness that God sees "the real me." We so easily make the mistake of basing our success on what others say about us and how well we seem to be doing in comparison to everyone else at church, but God doesn't evaluate us on those criteria. He evaluates us on what is working on the inside of us. He sees differently than man sees and He evaluates differently than man does. Man looks at the outward appearance, but God looks at the heart (1 Samuel 16:7). He doesn't define us by what we accomplish in our own strength, but by our secret thoughts and the inner workings of our hearts. The question we should ask is not "What do other people think of me?" but "What is heaven's perspective on my life?"

When we understand and accept that what God thinks about us is all that matters, it shatters the secret, ripening sin in our hearts and silences our urges to gratify the flesh. As our lives are brought into the light, we repent and we embrace God's plan for how to live our lives. We stop living for the praise of men and women and start living for an audience of One. We find ourselves desiring to live in righteousness for God and God alone. Our whole lives begin to change. Our prayer lives become holy, our fasting becomes holy, our giving becomes holy, our conversations become holy. Our thoughts, words and deeds are saturated in our awareness of the One who is above all.

Reality and Deception

Having the fear of the Lord means being in agreement with what God esteems highly and sharing His perspective. At IHOP, we often pray prayers like, "Lord, shock me now, instead of shocking me later, on the day Jesus judges the secret thoughts of our hearts." I believe that on the Day of Judgment, many who seemed outwardly successful in the things of the Spirit or appeared righteous to others will be found lacking as Jesus lays their hearts bare. What we do in secret and what we think in the secret places of our hearts—both righteousness and sin—will be weighed on that day and will impact how we spend eternity. In God's mercy, He has instructed us through His Word how to seek the value system of heaven and the fear of the Lord while we are on earth. He has given us advance notice so we have every opportunity to do life His way. He shocks us today so that we will not be shocked by His righteous judgments on the Day of Judgment; we will have lived in agreement with His way all along.

It is right that we live our lives in light of the judgment seat and of eternity, not by what people say about us. Unfortunately, we humans have a great propensity to be influenced by the latter and must constantly guard against it. When Jesus referred to drunkenness (Luke 21:34), He wasn't only referring to physically being intoxicated, although that is included. A person who is drunk is unaware and out of touch with reality. For example, a guy may get drunk at a party and think everyone considers him really cool; in reality, they think he is acting like a clueless dork. Being out of touch with reality is also called deception. Jesus explicitly highlighted this danger in the Olivet Discourse concerning the end of the age. He said, "Take heed that no one deceives you" (Matthew 24:4).

We must heed Jesus' words and violently and aggressively guard our hearts, minds, thoughts and deeds. Through the prophet Jeremiah, the Lord spoke about this issue in a time when the people were deluded about the reality of God: "The heart is deceitful above all things, and desperately wicked; who can know it? I, the Lord, search the heart, I test the mind, even to give every man according to his ways, according to the fruit of his doings" (Jeremiah 17:9-10).

God Sees and Acts

The fear of the Lord exposes our false ideas of a god made in our own image, instead of the reality of the eternal, living God. Whether we admit it or not, most of us have created a God that suits us—we select the passages that we like from the Bible and disregard those we don't; we choose to discuss spiritual matters with only those people who will agree with us and tell us what we want to hear; we readily accept the mercy, forgiveness and grace of God, but convince ourselves that God's call to holiness, righteous living and self-sacrifice doesn't apply to us. The fear of the Lord is the cure for our false views of God.

Wrong ideas about God are not new; they've been around for ages. The Israelites lacked the awareness of God as He truly is, which caused them to continually be unfaithful to Him. The Israelites viewed God as distant, detached and far-removed from them. They gave lip service to Him and used all the right words and phrases, but they had no fear of the Lord. As a result, they pursued and bowed down to other gods. They worshipped idols, the work of their own hands. They were under the dangerous false impression that God did not notice or mind their idolatry—that He turned His head as His chosen people gave their worship to false gods. Jeremiah called this "casual harlotry" (Jeremiah 3:9). The covenant God had made with His people was a marriage covenant—they were committing adultery as well as idolatry.

They were out of touch with reality. They thought because they were the people of God and because they knew a lot about God, they were excused from the heart-searching, soul-piercing reality of God. The Israelites believed they would always be blessed because they were the people of the covenant. They assumed God wouldn't care if they were unfaithful. They didn't believe He would judge them. They rested in a false peace, supposing God would not require them to repent or to face their sin. They said in their hearts, "You will not require an account" (Psalm 10:13).

The nation's apostasy was directly linked to wrong thoughts about God. They were comfortably settled in their complacency and unbelief. They unwisely placed their confidence in the false idea that they could be the people of the covenant without the covenant working in their lives. The Lord saw and said to Ezekiel the prophet, "Son of man, have you seen what the elders of the house of Israel do in the dark, every man in the room of his idols? For they say, 'The Lord does not see us, the Lord has forsaken the land'" (Ezekiel 8:12).

Even most of the prophets fed the people's unbelief. "They have lied about the Lord, and said, 'It is not He. Neither will evil come upon us, nor shall we see sword or famine.' And the prophets become wind" (Jeremiah 5:12). The prophets, who were supposed to shepherd Israel and communicate God's heart to the people, were rendered worthless by their deceiving ideas about God.

In contrast, the true prophets, such as Elijah, Jeremiah, Ezekiel, Joel and Zephaniah, preached the fear of the Lord. They cried out that God was near, that He did see and know and care about what the people did. They warned that He would not tolerate their idolatry and adultery, that there would be consequences if the people did not turn back to Him. They emphasized God's commitment to His people and that the God of mercy was also the God of judgment: if Israel repented, He would welcome her back, but if she continued in her harlotry, He would send judgment on the land. God had made it clear from the beginning that He is a jealous God and a jealous Husband. He is the God of blazing holiness who will not ignore His people just because they ignore Him.

God judged Israel countless times for their sins. Sometimes they would repent and follow Him for a while, but they always slid into complacency and compromise again, forgetting the truth of who God is. The Israelites did not learn from this continual cycle; they had no understanding of a God who could not tolerate sin and who would actually send judgment upon His chosen people. God's heart was broken by their unbelief. He longed for His people to come back to the true knowledge of Him. "Return, O backsliding children," He pleaded, "for I am married to you" (Jeremiah 3:14).

The prophet Joel cried out to the people of Israel, telling them to return to the Lord, to truly repent in their hearts: "Rend your heart, and not your garments; return to the Lord your God" (Joel 2:13). The only way they could return to the Lord was by learning the fear of the Lord and repenting of their wrong thoughts of God. Joel continued, "For He is gracious and merciful, slow to anger, and of great kindness; and He relents from doing harm" (Joel 2:14). Joel emphasized God's nature because the people had forgotten who He was. They could only exchange their wrong ideas about God for right ones if they knew what the right ones were. Because they had forgotten who God had declared Himself to be during the exodus from Egypt (Exodus 34), Joel reminded them.

The Lord also spoke through the prophet Zephaniah: "I will search Jerusalem with lamps, and punish the men who are settled in complacency, who say in their heart, 'The Lord will not do good, nor will He do evil'" (Zephaniah 1:12). The true prophets exposed the people's secret false beliefs about God and called them to repentance and to the fear of the Lord. They preached the real God, the living God. The prophetic spirit, in its purest form, is the declaration and manifestation that God is alive—that He sees, knows, hears, feels and acts, all for the sake of love.

In a dark hour of idolatry, the prophet Elijah confronted the people with the reality of the living God. He faced Israelites who had turned away from God and were worshipping Baal, a foreign god. Both Elijah and the idolaters set out to prove whose god was real. Each side prepared sacrifices and called on their god to send fire from heaven to burn up the sacrifice. The idolaters cried out to Baal many times throughout the day, but he did not answer. Elijah drenched his sacrifice with water and then prayed one time. He said, "Hear me, O Lord … that this people may know that You are the Lord God, and that You have turned their hearts back to You again" (1 Kings 18:36). Fire fell from heaven and consumed the sacrifice, the wood, the stones of the altar, and the water Elijah had poured over the altar. "Now when all the people saw it, they fell on their faces; and they said, 'The Lord, He is God! The Lord, He is God!'" (1 Kings 18:39). The fear of the Lord fell upon them as they realized that the Lord truly was alive and active.

Whenever true prophets like Elijah showed up on the scene, they brought this revelation—that God was very much involved in and concerned with Israel's affairs. Though generations of Israelites have spent their lives running from that reality, God has refused to be forgotten completely by them.

Embarking on the pursuit of God and committing ourselves to it for life will bring us more and more deeply into the right understanding of God and the true knowledge of God. It will tear down our false views of Him and remind us continually that He sees and acts.

Our Choices in Light of Eternity

So what does it mean, practically speaking, that God sees and acts? We have seen that He who sits on the judgment seat will examine the things we have done, whether good or bad, and that our choices will have consequences in the age to come. How does knowing that affect our daily actions and decisions? Paul told us that each one of our works—for or against God—in this age will be tested by fire. God will show us whether our earthly lives produced anything of lasting value:

> Now if anyone builds on this foundation with gold, silver, precious stones, wood, hay, straw, each one's work will become clear; for the Day will declare it, because it will be revealed by fire; and the fire will test each one's work, of what sort it is. (1 Corinthians 3:12-13)

The foundation is our salvation; it cannot be burned up or destroyed. But everything that we do for the Kingdom will be tested to see if we have done it with pure motivations—if we have been faithful servants (Matthew 25:19,23). God's reward system is based on whether or not we acted with eternity in mind. We cannot earn salvation by our works, but He will reward or judge each one of us differently according to our works. Daniel compared this reward system to the light of the stars. Each star looks different—it has a different color, a different magnitude of brightness. In a similar way, we will find that different people will forever shine with different degrees of righteousness.

> Many of those who sleep (*who have died*) ... shall awake, some to everlasting life, some to shame and everlasting contempt. Those who are wise shall shine like the brightness of the firmament and those who turn many to righteousness like the stars forever and ever. (Daniel 12:2-3, parenthetical comment added)

I would invite you to consider the eternity of God. Remember how we meditated on eternity in Chapter 1? Now consider your life after this age. You and I will never die. The choices we make in this age will affect how we spend eternity. Our words, deeds, thoughts and attitudes of the heart affect our quality of life in the age to come.

We will live forever in the consequences of our decisions.

Everything will be laid bare before God. We may be able to fool people here on earth, but there is no fooling God. One day we will stand before Jesus, the most honest Man who ever lived, and give an account for how we lived our lives. The Father has committed all judgment to His Son, and Jesus will judge and examine us based on the secret thoughts and beliefs of our hearts when we walked the earth. "In the day when God will judge the secrets of men by Jesus Christ" (Romans 2:16), His eyes will look right through all the fluff of our lives and He will declare the truth about us.

What is so glorious is that God has always given us the freedom to choose how we will spend eternity. It's why He put the tree of the knowledge of good and evil in the garden. He gives us the honor and dignity of deciding if we are for or against Him and His ways. God wants voluntary lovers. He will never force anyone to love Him or His ways, but He does make it clear that our choices have consequences. If you're not for God, you're against Him. If you're not a voluntary lover, you're a voluntary resister. There's no middle or neutral ground with God.

We only get one shot at this. We each have seventy or eighty years to live in light of all eternity and to choose whether or not to live in the fear of the Lord. Every single choice we make about what to look at, what to say, what to focus our thoughts on, how to spend our money and our time, how to treat our family and friends, is a choice that matters to God and will affect our quality of life in eternity. Choosing unrepentant sinfulness has eternal significance just as much as choosing righteousness and holiness.

I want to live in the fear of the Lord and in light of the judgment seat because I don't want to miss out on any of the reward God has for me. This doesn't mean we're supposed to walk around being afraid all the time. It means we make wise choices, repent when we sin, respond in humility when we are wrong, and ask God to help us in our weakness, all the while keeping eternity as our focus. Paul lived in this reality:

Therefore we make it our aim, *whether present or absent*, to be well pleasing to Him. For *we must all appear before the judgment seat* of Christ, that each one may receive the things done in the body, according to what he has done, whether good or bad. *Knowing, therefore, the terror of the Lord,* we persuade men; but we are well known to God, and I also trust are well known in your consciences. (2 Corinthians 5:9-11, emphasis added)

Good and Faithful Servants

Those who have the fear of the Lord are faithful with what the Lord has given them. They are good stewards of what He has entrusted to their care, no matter how big or small these gifts or responsibilities seem to them. Many of us will be surprised to find out when we stand before God how delighted and pleased He is with the millions of tiny things we did in our lives that we didn't think were a big deal—the small acts of service that nobody else knew about; the many silent prayers we prayed that nobody else heard; the times we made godly choices and didn't tell anyone. Every seemingly insignificant thing we do is significant to God. And He highly values things that we have done, not for the praise of men or for honor, but for God. He loves it when we are faithful even with the smallest things He has given us.

Being faithful to our words and promises is one area that many people consider a small responsibility. But understanding the fear of the Lord is letting your "yes" mean "yes" and your "no" mean "no" (Matthew 5:37). It means doing what you say you will do. It means being faithful to the promises you make to your children, faithful in prayer and in forgiveness, and faithful in giving your money, time and energy. The fear of Lord makes everything sacred—no longer do we label some things "sacred" and other things "secular." When we have the fear of the Lord, our entire lives and all our job assignments here on earth are holy before the Lord. David stated, "The fear of the Lord is clean, enduring forever" (Psalm 19:9).

Matthew 25 records a parable Jesus gave concerning how our faithfulness in this age affects our destiny in the age to come. In the parable, a master entrusted three of his servants with different amounts of talents (money). The talents speak of their (our) God-given influence or potential impact in this age, whether it be leading, pastoring, teaching, finances, time or any other resource or gift. Two of the servants were faithful with what they had been given. They used their gifts well and created profit for their master. The master told both of the men who had been faithful, "Well done, good and faithful servant; because you have been faithful over a few things, I will make you ruler over many things. Enter into the joy of your lord" (Matthew 25:21,23).

The third man took his one talent and hid it. He didn't want to use it to benefit his master. He was full of fear because he had a false image of his master, and he let that wrong fear create a victim mentality in him. He said, "Lord, I knew you to be a hard man, reaping where you have not sown, and gathering where you have not scattered. And I was afraid, and went and hid your talent in the ground" (Matthew 25: 24-25). The master rebuked this servant, made him give up the little that he had, and cast him away.

In order for us to be able to walk in faithfulness and the right fear of the Lord, we have to have a right understanding of God. He is not a hard task master. He is generous, kind, patient, loving and merciful; His yoke is light. We just have to be trustworthy with the time, energy, resources and finances that the Lord has given us. "Moreover it is required in stewards that one be found faithful" (1 Corinthians 4:2).

We are all given different amounts of resources and varied talents, abilities and gifts. We must be faithful with what we have, whether large or small, little or much. Apostles, prophets and evangelists are not more important than factory workers or housewives because their giftings and talents place them in the public eye. Each us has job assignments given by God, and we are meant to do them with excellence, perseverance and faithfulness. It's not what we've been given that matters; it's what we do with what we've been given that counts. The ones who have been faithful with a small amount of influence or knowledge on this earth will have more in the age to come than those who had much but were not faithful with it.

If we are faithful and walk in the fear of the Lord, we can have confidence that we will begin the lifelong journey into the true knowledge of God. We will taste, touch, hear and encounter the deep things of God in His Word. We will start to understand His countless, endless attributes: the greatness of His eternity, wisdom, goodness, immutability and self-sufficiency; His grace, mercy, justice, love and wrath; His patience, power, righteous dominion, omnipresence and omniscience. We will begin to awaken to the inexhaustible riches of the realm of the Spirit.

The reward is magnificent and endless. The way is simple. I'm astounded by the clarity and simplicity of the call laid out in Proverbs 2. We will not be able to stand before God and say, "You made the path too difficult or too unclear." The path to knowledge costs everything, but it's not too mysterious or difficult to find. It's as simple as this: if we apply these realities to our lives, we will have begun the journey of finding Him. We will begin to understand the fear of the Lord and find the knowledge of God.

CHAPTER

What Shall We Cry?

Spiritual leaders are called to know God and contend for His presence. The Church's greatest need right now is for spiritual leaders who are living according to the Proverbs 2 mandate. The Church and the world are in need of leaders who have the true knowledge of God and who understand the fear of the Lord.

Shut It Down

Spiritual leaders who claim to know God, but do not have living understanding of Him, are committing a serious offense against God. Leonard Ravenhill said in his book, *Why Revival Tarries*, "This generation of preachers is responsible for this generation of sinners" (p. 110).

One of God's primary criteria for sending judgment on a people or nation is negligence on the part of spiritual leaders. He said in Jeremiah's time:

> *The priests did not say, "Where is the Lord?" and those who handle the law did not know Me; the rulers also transgressed against Me; the prophets prophesied by Baal,*

and walked after things that do not profit. Therefore, I will bring charges against you. (Jeremiah 2:8-9, emphasis added)

How could the ones who spent the most time around the Word of God not know the God of the Word? How could the spiritual leaders of Israel not seek His face or even sense if His presence was with them? God told Jeremiah: "They did not know Me." They did not search for living understanding. The machine of the daily sacrifices kept running, the Temple did business as usual, but nobody realized that God was gone. How could the priests not notice God was gone?

And what about us? What about our church leaders? Is our machine of religion humming away, lulling us into the delusion that because we are present at church every Sunday for an hour or two, God's presence is there? We're pumping out sermons and Sunday school curricula and worship songs and church growth models and conferences and training seminars—the list goes on and on. There is no question that the Western Church knows how to do church. *But do we really know God?*

We are spiritually barren. We don't have the knowledge of God and we don't have the fear of the Lord—and only a few are even in pursuit of these. Our churches and cities and families aren't turning back to God. It doesn't matter how many Bible schools we have, how many church plants we have, or how many television and radio ministries we have. *Our cities are not turning back to God.* In fact, they appear to be going in the opposite direction. When those who are dying, sick, troubled, hurting, addicted, abused and abandoned show up at the doors of the Church, we are not able to help them. We can't heal, deliver, cure or comfort them. It takes the power of God to do that. And we don't have the power of God, the presence of God or the knowledge of God. All we can do is give them a hug, sign them up for a home group and hope for the best. Things will not get better because we use the latest evangelism method or create a better radio commercial, because at the end of the day, only the presence and power of God can affect eternity.

The prophet Malachi lived in a time similar to ours. The people brought impure, half-hearted sacrifices and meaningless worship before God because they did not know Him. The Lord cried out through Malachi, "Who is there even among you who would shut the doors, so that you would not kindle fire on My altar in vain? I have no pleasure in you ... nor will I accept an offering from your hands" (Malachi 1:10). Through Hosea He said, "For I desire mercy and not sacrifice, and the knowledge of God more than burnt offerings" (Hosea 6:6).

I believe the Lord is telling us: "Shut it down!" We cannot continue in our ministries if we aren't driven by the knowledge of God. It's time we discarded our definitions of success and impact and called people to get rooted and grounded in the knowledge of God. This call will be costly. We will lose people and finances; there will be those who choose not to pursue the knowledge of God. But it is God before whom we will stand, not our fellow believers, to give account one day. We can respond to this call now or later. We can store up eternal wealth or not. We can stand at the judgment seat and hear Jesus say, "Well done," or we can hear Him tell us that most of our ministries had no eternal value.

Let's stop the madness of the machine we call "the Church" and get back to the pursuit of wisdom. Let's call people to the knowledge of God. Let's labor to prepare the harvest for eternity.

Sent Laborers

Matthew 9 describes Jesus looking at the multitudes and seeing that they were like scattered, weary, leaderless sheep. He said to His disciples, "Pray the Lord of the Harvest that He would send out laborers into the harvest" (Matthew 9:37). Those laborers and shepherds are born, nurtured and matured in the place of prayer, intercession, and the knowledge of God.

I am contending for a sending from heaven as in the days of the prophets. Moses had the encounter with the burning bush; Isaiah saw the High and Lofty One in the temple; Ezekiel saw visions of God on His throne; the hand of the Lord touched Jeremiah's mouth; and John the Baptist was sent from God to bear witness of the Son. These people knew that they had been commissioned by God with the true knowledge of Him, something so deep that it would prepare their souls for the persecution and trials that they later encountered.

Not one of the heroes of the Christian faith received anything easily or quickly from the Lord. These laborers died a thousand deaths before the time we heard their stories. They gave up everything for the sake of their commission. Noah prophesied for 120 years that judgment was coming, and no one but his family believed him. Moses was in the desert for forty years before he encountered the burning bush. John the Baptist lived alone in the wilderness from his youth. Jesus was completely hidden for the first thirty years of His life. Paul endured three days of being blind and alone, facing his shattered paradigms, before he was entrusted with the Gospel—and then he spent three years in deep training before he began to preach (Galatians 1:15-18). Paul wrote of the commissioning process in 1 Thessalonians 2:4: "But as we have been approved by God to be entrusted with the gospel, even so we speak, not as pleasing men, but God who tests our hearts."

We so casually talk about being a shepherd, a messenger or a minister. We have cheapened the requirements of spiritual leadership to having a four-year degree and knowing some information about God. God trains His leaders by taking them into the furnace of prayer, killing them, and raising them up in Christ. This call to leadership is not something to be taken lightly. As "servants of Christ and stewards of the mysteries of God" (1 Corinthians 4:1), we need to approach our calling with holiness and godly fear. We are to be a people set apart as vessels for His manifestation.

We've established that having the true knowledge of God does not equal having facts that we have gathered concerning God. The true knowledge of God is the manifestation of Christ in a people— people who know the love of Christ in a manner that causes them to live it and act it out. They don't just talk about it or meditate on it—they manifest it. Paul prayed that we would know "the exceeding greatness of His power toward us who believe" (Ephesians 1:19). This knowing is a living manifestation of power in us and through us; it is the life and ministry of Christ lived out through earthen vessels. We embody the passions, the longings, the intents and the will of God. We express the heart of God to the ones who have not yet found the true knowledge of God.

Jeremiah prophesied that in the latter days God would raise up laborers who would minister to Him, manifest His heart and teach others how to know Him: "Return, O backsliding children ... for I am married to you ... I will give you shepherds according to My heart, who will feed you with knowledge and understanding" (Jeremiah 3:14-15). John the Baptist said, "He who has the bride is the bridegroom; but the friend of the bridegroom, who stands and hears him, rejoices greatly because of the bridegroom's voice" (John 3:29). The friends of the Bridegroom are the shepherds. They know that the Bride (the Church) belongs to the Bridegroom (Jesus). Their job is to encounter the Bridegroom (hear His voice) and to feed the people on the revelation of His heart. I am talking about the Word made flesh—Jesus—who gives weight to the message that comes out of our mouths. "The lips of the priest should keep knowledge" (Malachi 2:7). This is the call of spiritual leaders: to feed people on the manifestation of God.

We need leaders who know God and what He is saying. The true apostolic witness is more than being over a network of churches or of having great leadership abilities. We don't need just a little bit more in our ministries, in our churches and in our lives; we need something from another age. It's the hour for a people to be sent by heaven. It's the hour for Christ and the manifestation of His life in us.

The Hour in Which We Live

We are not called to the knowledge of God and to spiritual leadership in a vacuum. We are living in what I believe is the generation of the Lord's return. This generation will witness the greatest outpouring of the Holy Spirit and the greatest harvest of souls in all of history. We will also see the rage of Satan reach its height, the greatest manifestation of mankind's hatred of God, and the pinnacle of both God's judgment and mercy.

I don't have time to go into a detailed study of the End Times. (If you're interested in learning more about the hour in which we live, you should read Dave Sliker's book, *End-Times Simplified*, which is also in the Onething Reality book series.) I will just say that while there are more than 80 chapters in the Bible that speak about Jesus' first coming, there are more than 100 chapters that speak about His second coming. We cannot know the exact hour of His return. We *can* know the season. Jesus commanded us to watch and be ready: "Watch therefore, for you do not know what hour your Lord is coming ... be ready, for the Son of Man is coming at an hour you do not expect" (Matthew 24:42,44).

Jesus told us what this hour would be like: "But as the days of Noah were, so also will the coming of the Son of Man be" (Matthew 24:37). During Noah's time, mankind had reached such depths of wickedness that every thought and intent was wicked. The most merciful thing that God could do at that time was send a flood on the earth that would wipe the slate clean, giving mankind another chance. Jesus said the hour preceding His second coming would be like Noah's generation. This generation would reach even lower depths of wickedness and even higher heights of God's mercy. To survive the End Times and not become offended at God, we must truly know His heart.

Jesus said that many would become offended, not just during the coming judgments, but during the revival (Matthew 24:10). My friend Dave Sliker recently spoke about the great end-time outpouring of the Spirit in Joel 2:28. We tend to think that once the Spirit is poured out, everyone will gladly choose to believe in God. Sadly, when the Holy Spirit is poured out, mankind's hatred of God will come to the forefront. The fact is that, in the face of signs, wonders, miracles and righteous judgments, most will rage and rebel against God. Paul spoke about how people will willfully suppress and reject the true knowledge of God:

> What may be known of God is manifest in them, for God has shown it to them. For since the creation of the world His invisible attributes are clearly seen, being understood by the things that are made, even His eternal power and Godhead, so that they are without excuse, because, although they knew God, they did not glorify Him as God, nor were thankful, but became futile in their thoughts, and their foolish hearts were darkened ... and even as they did not like to retain God in their knowledge, God gave them over to a debased mind, to do those things which are not fitting. (Romans 1:19-22,28)

We see humanity's rejection of God laid out in Revelation 9-10, but we also see God's mercy strategy for that time: He will raise up prophetic messengers like Noah who will proclaim the knowledge of God.

Prophetic Messengers at the End of the Age

The message we will carry in the midst of judgment and mercy is the truth about God. Our words will either cut people to the heart, leading to their salvation, or it will harden them in their rebellion, leading to their damnation. The majority will turn away from the message. Either way, the truth we speak will expose and solidify the secret thoughts of the heart.

When God commissioned Isaiah as a prophetic messenger, He told him openly that only a few might hear and respond and be saved. Most of the people to whom he would preach had hard hearts and would reject the message:

Go, and tell this people: "Keep on hearing, but do not understand; keep on seeing, but do not perceive." Make the heart of this people dull, and their ears heavy, and shut their eyes; lest they see with their eyes, and hear with their ears, and understand with their heart, and return and be healed. (Isaiah 6:9-10)

This is the calling of prophetic messengers. We have to enter into spiritual leadership with open eyes and understand the reality of the situation.

Why is the prophetic message controversial, both inside and outside of the church? Because the prophetic messengers will ultimately proclaim a coming storm—a coming crisis being orchestrated by our God and administrated by our Jesus. Jesus is not coming back in the way that He left. He's coming back as a righteous judge. He's coming back to wage war on everything that opposes Him. He is going to refine the Bride (the Church and Israel) through the Great Tribulation. He will literally slaughter all those who have persecuted His Bride and who stand in the way of righteousness. The meek and silent Man described in Isaiah 53 is described ten chapters later as a warrior drenched in the blood of His enemies. "Their blood is sprinkled upon My garments, and I have stained all My robes," Jesus says, "for the day of vengeance is in My heart, and the year of My redeemed has come" (Isaiah 63:3-4). This doesn't sound like the Jesus everyone learned about in Sunday school, does it? Those who have taken the journey into the intimate knowledge of God's heart will be able to proclaim His true nature as the One who sees and acts, the One who is jealous for those who belong to Him.

We will not only speak about God's nature and proclaim the knowledge of God to the nations. We will speak comfort to Israel in her time of greatest crisis. Isaiah 40 records God's command to people to proclaim comfort to Jerusalem, even as all other nations surround her and plot to destroy her. God will raise up a prophetic people to proclaim that He has not forsaken Israel. Even now, God is orchestrating all of the events that will lead up to and will be included in the final phase of history in this age. He will come to fight for His people and to deliver them from their enemies. In Isaiah 40 we read that Israel and the nations around her will be confronted with the eternity of God, and fear and dread will come to those who had conspired against the Lord:

> The voice said, "Cry out!" And he said, "What shall I cry?" "All flesh is grass, and all its loveliness is like the flower of the field … The grass withers, the flower fades, but the word of our God stands forever." (Isaiah 40:6-8)

This chapter is about the revelation of God as Creator and speaks of His eternity and His freedom to do whatever He wants without hindrance. Prophetic messengers will confront the earth with this truth, although many will not accept it.

Isaiah 40 also indicates what will sustain and spiritually feed these laborers: the knowledge of God—the understanding of His eternity, sovereignty, wisdom, power and knowledge. I'm convinced the comforters Isaiah 40 prophetically spoke about are alive and being prepared right now. They will lay hold of God and contend for what is on His heart. They will come forth out of the darkness as burning and shining lamps. Their voices will declare the truth about God. They will not echo the message of the latest Christian books or teaching tapes from popular speakers. Their message will be one formed in and birthed from their experiential knowledge of God. When we ask God, "What shall I cry?" (Isaiah 40:6), this is more than a passive wondering about what to say. It is an active pursuit of a prophetic cry.

The apostle John laid hold of the end-time message (the little book in Revelation 10). We are meant to go after this message, as seen in Ezekiel 3:

> Now when I looked, there was a hand stretched out to me; and behold, a scroll of a book was in it. Then He spread it before me; and there was writing on the inside and on the outside, and written on it were lamentations, and mourning

and woe. Moreover He said to me, "Son of man, eat what you find; eat this scroll, and go, speak to the house of Israel." So I opened my mouth, and he caused me to eat that scroll. (Ezekiel 2:9–3:2)

Like John, Ezekiel became the oracle of the Lord. The message he proclaimed didn't come from information he knew intellectually. It came from who he was. By eating the scroll, he became one with the message.

We are called to take the message of the truth about God by force. We do this by living a lifestyle of prayer, fasting and diligent study of God's Word. We will eat and digest the Word of God. The message will taste sweet when we initially accept it. But it will begin to taste bitter as we begin to understand why God spoke to Isaiah as He did in Isaiah 6. However, we will not reject the message, because we will know God. We will consume His message until it possesses us; until we become His vessels and His oracles. We will truly become prophetic messengers at the end of the age.

The Pursuit of the Holy

Christians long to hear of God and to know Him. They may not verbalize it or even fully realize it, but deep down they know something is missing, and most of them know it's the true knowledge of God. They are asking, "What is He like? What is He doing? How does He feel? What do I mean to Him?" What would happen if one of the seraphim were to show up in one of our pulpits next week to answer our questions? One of the burning ones, one who has meditated on the knowledge of God for eternity—what do you think he would tell us? Tozer said, "Would he not charm and fascinate his hearers with rapturous descriptions of the Godhead? And after hearing him … would we not thereafter demand of those who presume to teach us that they speak to us from the mount of divine vision, or remain silent altogether?" (The Knowledge of the Holy, p. 71).

What would it be like if the knowledge of God burned in us like it does in the seraphim? Imagine being so on fire with living understanding of God that all you have to do is declare the Scriptures that exalt God and proclaim His name—and people get radically healed and saved, are filled with the Holy Spirit, and run to the altar to commit their hearts to the lifelong journey of knowing Him.

I'm desperate to be among a company of people—preachers, singers, musicians and intercessors—who have eaten the scroll; who are possessed by the Word of God; who pursue and proclaim the knowledge of God with all that is in them. Daniel saw that "the people who know their God shall be strong and carry out great exploits" (Daniel 11:32). I'm consumed by this vision of people who know God—*for real.*

I'm convinced that God will raise up people who manifest the knowledge of God. It doesn't matter whether you used to be an alcoholic, drug dealer or prostitute, or if you've gone to church your entire life. Anyone can commit to seeking the knowledge of God and to the lifestyle of a prophetic messenger.

All over the earth right now, people are giving themselves to lifestyles of prayer, fasting and digesting the Word of God for the purpose of that Word becoming flesh in them. Being refined in the hidden place strips them of their titles, their reputations and their entitlements, and causes them to confront their spiritual barrenness, the arguments and lies that constitute their shallow knowledge of God. Then they begin to enter into the true knowledge of God, into the glorious intimacy with God that is available to all who hunger. What happens to these people when they have gone on the journey described in Proverbs 2? What kind of messenger emerges from the wilderness of prayer, fasting and meditation in the word of God?

I believe such people will come forth preaching with power, authority and clarity. They will feed the hungry on the true knowledge of God, leading them to the paths of wisdom. Their message will shake cities all over the earth. Their lives will be more than memorized facts—their entire existence will scream of the reality of God Himself.

I challenge you to join these messengers. Take the path of wisdom laid out in Proverbs 2. It is not difficult to find, and the reward is certain. The pursuit of the Holy—a lifestyle of prayer, fasting, and meditation on the Word—can only end in one way: "you will understand the fear of the Lord, and find the knowledge of God" (Proverbs 2:6).

Recommended Reading/References

Charnock, Stephen. *The Existence and Attributes of God.* Grand Rapids, MI: Baker Books, 1996.

Lake, John G. *John G. Lake: The Complete Collection of His Life Teachings.* Compiled by Roberts Liardon. New Kensington, PA: Whitaker House, 1999.

Ravenhill, Leonard. *Why Revival Tarries.* Minneapolis: Bethany House Publishers, 1987.

Saint John of the Cross. *The Collected Works of St. John of the Cross.* Trans. Kieran Kavanaugh and Otilio Rodriguez. Washington, D.C.: ICS Publications, 1991.

Tozer, A.W. *The Knowledge of the Holy.* San Francisco: HarperSanFrancisco, 1961.

von Balthasar, Hans Urs. *Prayer.* Trans. Graham Harrison. San Francisco: Ignatius Press, 1986.

What is the IHOP-KC Missions Base?

The IHOP-KC Missions Base is an international missions organization committed to:

- Prayer – intercession, worship, healing, prophecy, and other expressions
- Fasting – our fasting teams cover 365 days a year
- The Great Commission – proclaiming Jesus to all nations with power as the way to establish His justice in the Earth

Our work includes equipping and sending out missionaries as dedicated intercessors and anointed messengers who are working to see revival in the Church and a Great Harvest among the lost.

Please visit www.IHOP.org for more information about IHOP, joining our staff, or attending an internship, our Bible school or our music academy.

IHOP-KC Missions Base Vision Statement

To call forth, train and mobilize worshipping intercessors who operate in the forerunner spirit as end-time prophetic messengers. To establish a 24-hour-a-day Prayer Room in Kansas City as a perpetual solemn assembly that "keeps the sanctuary" by gathering corporately to fast and pray in the spirit of the Tabernacle of David as God's primary method of establishing justice—full revival unto the Great Harvest. To send out teams to plant houses of prayer in the nations after God grants a breakthrough of His power in Kansas City. The forerunner spirit operates in God's grace in context to the fasted lifestyle (Matthew 6) and prepares others to live in wholehearted love by proclaiming the beauty of Jesus as Bridegroom, King and Judge.

Visiting IHOP-KC on Weekends

Encounter God Services are held every Friday and Saturday at IHOP. We pray each of these services will release renewal, conviction, refreshing, impartation and equipping. On Friday nights, Mike Bickle teaches on themes related to intimacy with God. On Saturday nights, Mike Bickle teaches on themes related to the End Times.

Visit IHOP-KC at www.IHOP.org

The International House of Prayer Missions Base website has been designed for easy browsing. The following branches of the missions base have been incorporated into one cohesive website:

- IHOP
- Onething
- Children's Equipping Center
- Forerunner School of Ministry
- Forerunner Music Academy
- Joseph Company
- Events & Conferences
- Internships & Training Programs
- Omega Course

The website also offers a variety of services. Whether you are interested in visiting IHOP, receiving the Missions Base Podcast, browsing the bookstore, watching live Webcasts, or enrolling in FSM's online eSchool, the website delivers the information you need. With login capabilities that allow you access to more comprehensive IHOP materials, we hope our site will be a valuable resource for you. Website features include:

- Podcasting
- MP3 Downloads
- Forums
- Free & subscription-based Webcasts
- Sermon and teaching notes
- eSchool distance learning
- Internship applications
- Prayer room blogs
- Online bookstore
- And more!

1
onething

Onething is more than a conference.

It is a ministry committed to seeing a great awakening in the Body of Christ as the hearts of men and women come alive to the true nature of God.

Onething is a young adult ministry based at the International House of Prayer in Kansas City, Missouri. We at Onething have a specific message and carry a mandate to call young adults to return to their primary purpose in this life: loving Jesus. We endeavor to assist young adults in walking out the first commandment to love the Lord with all of their hearts, minds, souls and strength and to pursue a wholehearted passion for Jesus.

Our desire is for the truth of the Man Jesus to pierce hearts, remove chains of bondage, open eyes to understanding, revive complacent hearts, and ultimately cause young adults to become wholehearted lovers of Jesus Christ.

ONE THING HAVE I DESIRED, AND THAT WILL I SEEK ...
PSALM 27:4

WHAT DO YOU DESIRE?

www.IHOP.org

FORERUNNER SCHOOL OF MINISTRY

Redefining Theological Education
Through Night and Day Prayer

FOUR PROGRAMS:
- *Apostolic Preaching Program*
  Four-Year Program

- *Worship and Prayer Program*
  Four-Year Program

- *Healing and Prophecy Program*
  Two-Year Program

- *Biblical Studies Program*
  Four-Year Program

ONE ACADEMY:
- *Forerunner Music Academy*
  Three-Year Program

THREE INSTITUTES:
- *Joseph Company*
- *Apostolic Missions Institute*
- *Evangelist Institute*

CTEE:
- *e-School* – offering access to
  Video/Audio/Class Notes

CONTACT US:
12444 Grandview Road
Grandview, Missouri 64030

IHOP Internship Programs

IHOP offers a variety of three-month and six-month internships for all ages. Each internship has the same basic components, including prayer meeting attendance, classroom instruction, practical ministry experience, community fellowship and team building, conference participation, practical service, and Bible study. Internship attendees regularly participate in prayer meetings – between 15 and 25 hours a week – in the prayer room, which can include worship team involvement, intercession for revival, personal devotional time and study of the Word. Education and instruction cover a wide range of topics, including Christian foundations, prayer, worship, intimacy with God, the Bridal Paradigm of the Kingdom of God, the prophetic and healing ministries, serving the poor, and many others.

Intro to IHOP is a three-month internship for people of all ages, married or single, who want to learn and experience all that IHOP represents – prayer, worship, intimacy, etc.

Simeon Company is a three-month training program for people ages 50 and older who refuse to retire in their desire to radically serve Jesus through prayer, fasting, and worship.

One Thing Internship is a six-month daytime internship for young adults between the ages of 18 and 25 who are singers, musicians, intercessors or evangelists. This program includes housing and 18 meals a week.

Fire in the Night is a three-month nighttime internship for those between the ages of 18 and 30 who want to worship and minister to the Lord through the night, midnight to 6 a.m. This program includes housing and 18 meals a week.

Summer Teen Internship is a three-week summer program to equip teens in prophetic worship, intercession and intimacy with Jesus. Housing is provided with IHOP-KC families.

FOrErUNNEr MEDIa GrOUP Ⓕ

Music • Books • Television

Forerunner Media Group (FMG) is committed to providing the Body of Christ with books, music, teaching, and other resources that cause them to fall more deeply in love with God. It is our prayer that you will be blessed by the music, teachings, and books, and that you will be impacted at the heart level and grow in spiritual maturity as a result. Our desire is that our materials would stir you to abandon yourself to God in every way and enter into a lifestyle reflecting your understanding of God's infinite love for you and your response of devoted love to Him.

In addition to serving the Body of Christ, FMG serves the prayer movement, the IHOP missions base and IHOP's staff members. Our authors and artists—all of whom are on staff at IHOP— spend extended amounts of time in prayer, worship, fasting and studying the Word of God. They faithfully sit at the feet of Jesus and cry out for revelation of His heart. The worship leaders lead music sets at IHOP for many hours each week and saturate themselves in God's presence. Those who have authored books or produced teachings have dedicated themselves to hours of seeking understanding of the Scriptures and asking God to reveal His heart to them. The result is music that will minister to your heart as you minister to God's heart, and books and teachings full of profound insight from the Word of God.

Recent and Upcoming Music Releases Include:

Constant – A Collection from IHOP Worship Leaders
The World Can Wait – Merchant Band
Fading – Audra Lynn
Simply Beautiful – A Collection from the Women of IHOP
Longing for the Day – Julie Meyer
Always On His Mind – Misty Edwards

Recent Book Releases Include:

Pursuit of the Holy — Corey Russell
The Seven Longings of the Human Heart — Mike Bickle with Deborah Hiebert
The Omega Course: End Times Teaching — Mike Bickle
The Rewards of Fasting — Mike Bickle with Dana Candler
End-Times Simplified — David Sliker

PRAYER, FASTING AND THE GREAT COMMISSION
IHOP-KC ENDORSEMENTS

The Church today needs to be mobilized with continual prayer and fasting to release the harvest of souls waiting to be garnered from among the nations. Mike Bickle's reliable ministry at his Missions Base in Kansas City is helping to answer a great need in this hour.
— Jack W. Hayford, The Church On The Way

The Great Commission needs to be fueled with fiery continual prayer with fasting. Our greatest effectiveness in reaching millions of souls will be seen only as our work is bathed in prayer and fasting. Prayer ministries like Mike Bickle's in Kansas City are important for the completion of the Great Harvest.
— Bill Bright, Campus Crusade for Christ

The Great Harvest needs to be supplied by continual prayer and fasting. Intercessory ministries like Mike Bickle's in Kansas City are vital for the fulfillment of the Great Commission.
— Loren Cunningham, YWAM

As a lifelong missiologist, I cannot help but think that the landscape of humanity will drastically change when the body of Christ actually becomes a House of Prayer. Mike Bickle has risked it all to convince us of this fact. I heartily recommend this amazing work!
— C. Peter Wagner, Leadership Institute

Spiritual awakening in our nation and world cannot be sustained unless heaven's bowls stay continually filled through worship and intercession. Now more than ever, we need night and day prayer to make a difference! Thanks to Mike Bickle for helping to lead the charge.
— Dutch Sheets